D0193236

CHRONICLES ABROAD

St. Petersburg

Edited by John and Kirsten Miller

CHRONICLE BOOKS
SAN FRANCISCO

Printed in Singapore.

Library of Congress Cataloging-in-Publication Data:

St. Petersburg / edited by John and Kirsten Miller.

p.   cm. — (Chronicles Abroad)

ISBN 0-8118-0879-3

1. Saint Petersburg (Russia)—Literary collections.

2. Russian literature—Translations into English.

I. Miller, John, 1959-   . II. Miller, Kirsten, 1962-

III. Title: Saint Petersburg. IV. Series.

PN 6071.S16S7   1995

808.8'03247453—dc20   94-34287

CIP

Editing and design: Big Fish Books

Composition: Jennifer Petersen

Distributed in Canada by Raincoast Books,

8680 Cambie Street, Vancouver, B.C. V6P 6M9

10 9 8 7 6 5 4 3 2 1

Chronicle Books

275 Fifth Street

San Francisco, CA 94103

Special thanks to Maggie dePagter

Contents

Andrea Lee

EPIGRAPH

WHEN WE GOT to Leningrad, two weeks ago, the branches of the trees around the Winter Palace were still white with the famous hoarfrost of this damp region; above the frozen Neva, in the stunningly clear light of a minus-thirty-degree morning, the blue-green palace looked like the final step in a theorem proving that cold weather would be the eternal state of the world. As our taxi crossed the bridge to Vasilevsky Island, I saw people strolling on the ice of the river, all of them as bundled up

Andrea Lee is a regular contributor to the New Yorker. *This excerpt is from her 1984 collection of essays,* Russian Journal.

as I was in fur coats and hats and tightly wrapped scarves. (I've found that by far the best way to deal with temperatures below twenty degrees Fahrenheit is to wrap my face like a mummy until only my eyes show, and then to breathe the warmed air coming in through the cloth.) Far behind them, the gold spires of the Peter and Paul Fortress shone under the blinding sky like a signal to even colder countries, farther north.

Even then, the length of the days betrayed the approach of spring. Every day the twilight comes a bit later and hangs longer over the city, and in the afternoons, everyone, starved for light through the darkness of December and January, is out strolling along the streets and canals. After our arrival the weather swiftly grew warmer, the temperatures rising daily, until now the snow has turned to puddles of slush and it is possible to go outside in what Russians call a *"demi-saison"* (many of their fashion terms are French), a wool coat, instead of a fur or sheepskin. I paid careful attention to the Neva, so as not to miss the breakup of the ice. I imagined that I would be awakened one dawn by the fabled cracking sounds like gunfire that would mean that the river had wrestled itself free from winter. Instead, as I paused one sunny afternoon on the Dvortsovyi Bridge, I heard a light tinkling, like crystals in a chandelier, and looked down to see an open channel about two feet wide in the thick gray ice; inside was a swift eddy of brownish water where dozens of tiny pieces of ice were caught and ringing against one another. This delicate chiming seemed to be an apt voice for this ravishing artificial city of pastels, balanced on its marshes at the top of the world. The combination of Mediterranean colors and architectural shapes with the high white skies of the North gives Leningrad, to me, the disturbing glamour one finds in exotic hybrid fruits and flowers—wherever the hand of man has tampered outrageously with nature.

Nina Berberova

THE ITALICS ARE MINE

THE TRAIN CAME into the Finland Station. Here is Russia, my homeland, the return home, war. The first days of September 1914, thick dust, a crowd of recruits. The sadness, first felt by me in the soldiers' chorus: "They rose early in the morning—sounded the alarm." The alarm is here, above this troop train, droning with anxiety, half the sky in flames, a peal above the Neva—

Russian novelist Nina Berberova's novel, Kursiv Moi (The Italics Are Mine) recounts her childhood in St. Petersburg and Moscow. The Italics Are Mine was originally published in 1969; this excerpt is from a new translation by Phillipe Radley.

"Miss, give us a foreign charm for luck!"—I am giving him a small handbag mirror. It is strange that I have never valued my things, I can give them away, lose them, I have no "sacred" things as Russians did in the old days (spoon, comb). A clean towel and a clean pillowcase—this is all I need. The rest is unimportant. I give him the little mirror. His overcoat is rolled up and strapped over one shoulder.

A brass band bursts out unexpectedly, drowning the chorus. On the Liteiny Bridge lanterns burn. Why do they burn? Why does the cab driver sit sideways? Why does a woman cry? Why does a child ask: "Mister, give me a kopeck?" Why? Why does the policeman have such a fat stomach and the priest a still fatter one? Why does this boy, the son of our doorman, patter to my father: "They promised, Nikolai Ivanovich, but they didn't give it to me. It didn't work out." (This about a scholarship to a trade school.) Why everywhere: they didn't give it, it didn't turn out, it fell through, it fizzled out. Why? Why is it cold in September? Dark in October? Why does

Dasha have an embarrassed look and a black eye? "Got drunk yesterday before leaving and smashed me with his fist. They dispatched them to Galicia." What does all this mean? Why all this?

Wherever I look—at the ladybird the size of a house, children playing in the meadow, the papa and mama spreading out the white tablecloth or at those cows saying "moo," I see only one thing: sadness, poverty, "didn't work out," war, soldiers' boots, policemen's boots, generals' boots, cloudy sky over all this, the autumn sky of wartime Petersburg.

In a few days I return to school. The joy of meetings, a couple of new girls. Getting acquainted. "And who is that? She speaks to no one."—"That's Shklovskaya, she writes verse." I feel I am dying of curiosity mingled with desire to begin a friendship, and fear that my literary superiority has come to an end. She sits down next to me, to share the same desk. She, like me, is thirteen but her face is that of an adult: the serious look of grey eyes, the narrow nose, the slightly pursed lips, and the figure of a woman. Unintentionally I am flustered. We get on familiar terms, however. She says she has a cousin, a literary critic. I have never heard of him (I am embarrassed). I introduce her to Nadia Otsup, who has a poet brother; then I introduce her to Lucia M. (later shot), who has a publisher father. And also to Sonia R. (did away with herself in 1931), whose brother is a budding movie actor. We are all the cream of the class. She now is also the cream of the class. I allude to this, she understands me, but is silent.

In the Russian class she is called to the board. Is it true she writes verse? It is true. She is in no way embarrassed, she is calm as stone. Perhaps she will recite some to the class? Why, certainly she can! In her face no agitation at all. I worry for her. She looks at the ceiling and then through the window. Her brows, round and high, rise still higher. Assuredly, very distinctly, she speaks:

Ah, if only I could fly
From the earth into the sky
And forget those chains of lead
That my liberty impede.
Live in freedom, sorrowless,
Sing my song in happiness.

I inhale with difficulty. This is so beautiful I feel that all in me melts from rapture. Natasha continues to read:

But my efforts are in vain,
Swamps and dust and fog remain,
I am not allowed to rise,
I am forced to close my eyes,
Chains are heavy, I must wait,
But my time is late.

My heart beats wildly. I love her. I love her braid, the birthmark on her nose, her too white, adult hands, her little ring, her collar of lace. I love her face reminiscent of Cranach's madonna, and most of all I love her verse.

"Listen, Shklovskaya," I say to her casually during a break, "you have an ay-ay somewhere . . . "

"Yes? Where?"

" 'My eyes . . . ' "

"Ah! Good. I must revise it. I wrote it only yesterday. I didn't have time to check that it was all right."

I decide to reveal to her my most secret secret, about which I have said nothing to anyone. It is my secret and I am fearful, ashamed of admitting to it, and until now I have revealed it to no one. I tell her that I do not like *Eugene Onegin.* Why should one like it? At first Tatiana falls in love, without saying two words to the man, simply because of a look (foppish, boring, sated, empty). Then she marries a fat general simply because her mother asks her to, a mother who till a ripe old age is full of Grandisonianisms. Then Tatiana tells Onegin that she doesn't love him and chases him away—

what old-fashioned and irresponsible escapades . . . Natasha stands in front of me with a motionless expression: only her roundish brows are slightly raised and it's as if her lips were narrowed. She says: "Is this really important? Does it make any difference? What's important is that 'His beaver collar/Becomes silvery with frosty dust,' what's important is how the enjambments run on from line to line, from stanza to stanza. And the language! The irony! And Pushkin himself!"

I run home to be alone and think all this over. I sense that new perspectives are opening for me. That literature is turning a completely new side to me, a new level of meanings and ideas.

In the next four years that fate let her live until her arrest, we became friends. We exchanged rings, we gave each other our baptismal crosses. She was arrested for her membership in the S.-R. left group after the murder of the German ambassador Mirbach in Moscow in 1918. In prison she exchanged my cross of pure gold for a pack of cigarettes. I don't remember when her cross, which I never wore, was stolen, or by whom.

When we became friends, everything receded from me. She replaced everyone, all friendships. Together we discovered Wilde and Maeterlinck, Hamsun and Ibsen, Baudelaire and Nietzsche, Annensky, Tiutchev. We shared all that was ours in the present, as well as our entire past—in essence so poor, for we had not been together in it. Together we loved Ibsen's *Brand* and Wilde's *Dorian Gray* and Akhmatova's verse and Blok's *Snow Mask*, and in the summer we wrote long letters to each other daily, we exchanged verse, books. I was more spontaneous and more alive than she, but she was brighter, she knew everything (so it seemed to me then), I understood everything, she answered all questions. In this friendship there was no "older" and "younger," no "teacher" and "pupil"—there was equality, devotion to one another, an insatiable curiosity in each other. And beneath all was poetry, hers and mine.

In the second year of our relationship, changes occurred in her family that fundamentally altered her life. Till then she had lived with her mother and father in a small stuffy flat crammed with furniture in a low-middle-class neighborhood: in the entrance you couldn't get around the trunks and wardrobes. The old servant shuffled through the rooms in soft slippers, her toes, with long dirty nails, protruding through the holes. The flat smelled of cabbage, fish, onion—yellow, dim little lamps burned from the ceiling—and it was cold, crowded, restless. Her father slept in the study on a leather couch (a piece of bast stuck out of it), her mother somewhere on the other side of the kitchen, at the end of the dark corridor. She was a woman of about forty, heavily made up, with gypsy ear-rings hanging from her ears and curls burned by curling tongs on her forehead. I felt no sympathy towards her and only hid this with difficulty. Her father was a young-looking, ruddy, cheerful man with a light brown beard and grey wide-open eyes; he was always running somewhere, always hurrying, always doing things at speed. Then this life cracked and fell apart: Mr. Shklovsky, suddenly, taking Natasha with him, moved into a beautiful flat on Staronevsky Avenue, furnished it, hired a cook and a maid and began waiting for a divorce, to marry another. Something happened to him in his career of mechanical engineer that completely changed his financial status and along with it his family affairs. Natasha lived quite painfully through this whole crisis. Her mother quickly married a man who was somehow like herself—there was something in him unpleasant, not straightforward, and not wholly clean. Mr. Shklovsky took a wife who was beautiful, calm, affectionate, who dressed with taste and knew how to get along with everybody. She and Natasha had a good relationship. In all she was ten years older than we. It seems that all were happy with this new turn of affairs. And so was I.

I return to the first year of the war, which is called the "First," "One" "World" and "Great." Here I must speak of someone who together with Natasha Shklovskaya had a tremendous influence on me in those years.

Tatiana Adamovich, to whom Gumilev dedicated his "amorous" book, *The Quiver*, came to our school as a class monitor and a teacher of French. After the first lesson, as soon as the door closed behind her, I jumped up from my seat and cried out: "There's a Fury!"—not fully understanding what "Fury" meant, but this word, like "marquetry" once, pleased me by its sound and I had the need to shout it out. She heard it from the corridor. Later, one day, she asked me: "Why exactly did I then seem to you a Fury?" She was thinnish, dark-haired with large pale grey eyes, fine elegant hands and an unusual intonation in her speech, where *r* and *l* shaded into one another, and all *i* sounds were particularly sharp. She was from a special world: acquainted with Akhmatova and attending meetings of the Hyperboreus; in conversations with her I drank in every word. After class Natasha and I stayed in the teachers' study, that very room where once

Musia R. initiated me into the facts of life near a window covered with snow. Tatiana spoke with us about verse, acmeism, French poetry, Koussevitsky's concerts, about artists from The World of Art, Meyerhold, Mandelstam, Tsarskoe Selo and Volkonsky and his ballet school. Like poor Lazarus I gathered crumbs from the table where all these divinities feasted. In 1936 she came to Paris (after the Russian Revolution she ran a ballet school in Warsaw). I saw her. "Is that you?" she said, confused whether or not to be formal, and I remembered the lines of Gumilev about her:

> Dear one with a summer smile
> With fine, weak hands,
> And with dark hair perfumed
> Like the honey of two millennia.

Corridors, classrooms, halls—all was immersed in darkness. A lamp on the table was lit. Natasha and I sat on a leather couch, Tatiana walked from corner to corner, hands behind her back (she had this masculine habit), and spoke to us; we rhythmically turned our heads after her, to the right and left. Each word lodged in my memory like a playing card in a pack, and at night in bed, my head tucked under the blanket, I repeated her words as if laying out before me my whole motley pack. I marked the cards with my personal signs (there were not four suits, but an infinite number), and then again concealed them in my memory, as Gogol's Ikharev hid his in a suitcase. "All has been lost—and nothing has been lost!" I want to cry out to her now, if she is still alive. "All has perished, and nothing has perished!"

But, of course, the principal theme of her talks was Akhmatova. Of the two of us I, because of immaturity, imitated her a great deal at the time, and for me she was a special being. We read our own verse to Tatiana, and she spoke about what poetry was, of modern poetry, and the potentials of new Russian prosody beloved by the symbolists and the acmeists. Sometimes she took our verse and returned it to us in a week, saying she had read it to Akhmatova. She praised us quite rarely, but admitted that one of my poems was good. It ended:

Today my long-awaited
Thirteenth spring arrived.

"I will give it to my brother to read and he will say it is his. Only he will change 'thirteenth' to 'sixteenth.' " She laughed. Her brother, later the critic Georgy Adamovich, was then probably about twenty.

Tatiana's closest friend was the first wife of the acmeist poet Georgy Ivanov, Gabrielle, an airy, charming being, French by birth. This entire group of people, thanks to my constant thoughts about them, started in time to transform themselves in my imagination into a kind of magical Olympus: at first they appeared out of the fog, out of nothingness, then they acquired a shape, and then they began to lose the clarity of features when I gave them fantastic haloes that blinded my eyes. I lived in an astonishing, enticing world. An E in physics and an F in German sobered me for a moment, but again very quickly I sweetly and secretly plunged into another dimension, where there was neither physics nor German, but infinite bliss from poem to poem.

Yet what exactly did I like then in poetry? The possibility of doing what demi-gods were doing? Or of settling in a realm of abstract beauty? Of giving vent to Liebestraums inwardly muffled? Or did I strive to realize myself in the world? Apply myself to the sole art I thought I understood in those days? And how to grasp the beautiful? Was it feeling without thoughts? Primitive, animalistic—or passive, like a vegetable? I think all this was present; but especially the search for moments of anxiety, awe, and triumph.

Of the three realms—politics, ethics, and aesthetics—the first was the air of those years, the second the object of my protest, but the third remained alien. I felt that in the end it had to become bound up with my life, and that "aesthetic truth" sooner or later would be revealed to me. I knew it would not slip away from me, that I would find it, but meanwhile I could only humbly meditate on the difference between our pots and pans in which kasha was being served and that vase in which a painted woman, with fine hands and a knot of dark hair, kept corn or olive oil two thousand years ago. That basic and eternal feeling for measure and beauty—those who have not ached because of it in youth will remain deaf to it for life!

It doesn't reveal itself in discursive speech. It is hidden somewhere in a deep hiding-place in man: this place has nothing to do with noisy horrors and weird omens, with all that is petty and ridiculous which surrounds man outside like a night's drunken bout, thirty leagues from all that is dear. It has nothing to do with the predicament of the nocturnal world all around. Eternity can reveal itself at a bus stop; putting out a cigarette butt we suddenly understand the particularity of each separate human being; in front of a post office window the brittleness of the whole world "system" might flash at us; in a consulate reception room we find our own inescapable end bound up with a specific page of the calendar. There is that moment when an average man eats his average dinner, buys his average aspirin at the chemist— but in the following fraction of a second all that is average in him crumbles; his own particularity, the senselessness and wisdom of it all appears through his poor bald patch, in his glasses which slide down his sweaty nose—and we see a horizon without end.

I wandered all around the Karaulov house that summer; this was my farewell to it, and to the gardens where an alley of lime trees led out to the fields. Everything augured change, especially in the evenings when the whole village came to promenade through the orchards of this "nest of noblemen." Was this a premonition that in about two or three years these verandas and porches would gleefully burst into flames, and superintendents would circle convulsively, hung from apple trees? I do not know. But as soon as evening fell in the flower beds, near the ponds, alongside hammocks, in the arbor, shadows would flash by, a balalaika would be strummed, chords would be stretched out of the accordion. It seemed strange—and even now seems not altogether probable— that there was, so to speak, a "cramping" of the landowners several years before the Revolution. Yet at the same time there was something natural in this. Indeed, the peasants seemed to feel, what was there to wait for? Our best years, mind you, will pass while one sits waiting for changes in his izba and one can be sent away to bloody Galicia. Why not rock in hammocks in which no one has rocked for a long time anyway? Why not breathe of the lordly gillyflower: it will not harm them!

I wandered in the cemetery where Oblomov lay, where it seemed to me my consciousness had first emerged. Apple-tree branches, which once I was unable to reach, now touched the ground. The dry well which we yelled down so we could hear the echo was still the same, with a familiar half-rotted wood smell. Having looked into it once I remembered how I dreamt I would be thrown in. "I won't get out," I said to myself calmly, "I will remain there to die of thirst." But then, let's say on the third day, I suddenly notice that a spring has burst through at my very feet. It runs along, babbling and gleaming, and I bend down to drink. So I begin to live—at the bottom of the well, with a source that feeds me and which no one knows of in the world. What's most important is to find the source. In the well? In myself? Why? To live! Why live? Is this necessary? Yes, but only if the source is found. What source? I meant to say the spring. I am a spring too, a spring needs a spring to spring up. A spring is looking for a spring! What's most important is to find it. Because the well without fail will exist.

At that moment I suddenly understood my future, as if illumined by lightning: I saw that the well would be, that it already was. And that if I did not find the secret source in it, I would perish.

(And if snakes crawl out, I would find the pipe to charm them.)

I returned home late. In the dark garden young voices were yelling: "Vanka come! Mashka's waiting!" Waiting among the peasants there were the priest's daughters and others I had known since childhood.

I went to my room. The window opened onto the garden and a moon was rising over the old lime trees. For the first time I felt that a symbol rose, above me and my life, illuminated life and its meaning for me. Up to then all signs—even the comet I had asked for—were only signs, like the *a, b, c* in geometry that designate the angles or sides of a triangle. But now a symbol appeared full of meaning, there was the well and the source in it, about which I alone knew. And snakes. And a pipe. As if I had tasted of the tree of knowledge, the effect was no longer a pointless overflowing of the soul but great sadness.

(You could charm all the snakes with the pipe. But one old snake was stupid and deaf; it didn't hear the melody.)

This window always reminded me of that window in Otradnoe where Natasha and Sonya, who "did not concern me," whispered at night, while Prince Bolkonsky listened to them from downstairs. So my mother and the Decembrist's granddaughter who sometimes visited us surrendered themselves to dreams, while downstairs there was already someone who stirred their imagination. And Oblomov's daughters, Olga and Alina, entrusted each other with their secrets about passing hussars, their mother about uhlans of Nicholas I's time. But where was I in all of this? What was mine? I felt myself foreign to them all, unlike them, terribly far from their dreams, their whispers and hopes. I lit a candle, took *War and Peace* and wanted to find that passage about Natasha and Sonya but instead I found the chapter where Natasha dances at her uncle's after the hunt and the uncle's mistress (a serf) looks lovingly at her. This again seemed to me a kind of camouflage: the mistress should have hated Natasha, should have been mean to her; the children and grandchildren of this mistress were now laughing in the park, trampling the flowers—this was truth I understood, which I could accept in its entirety. They awaited the moment when they would tear the brocade from the walls of the drawing room and make blankets out of it for their children. They were right, and all that Tolstoy wrote was illusion; I couldn't believe in it, life rose between me and it with my own metaphor.

I looked at the full moon that had risen over the quiet gardens, my eyes filled up with tears, and something shook within me; I felt death (Grandfather had had a stroke the evening before) in the house, a death that was not terrible, but somehow natural and timely. I felt a strange weakness and then through tears saw a second full moon; it convulsively tried to overtake the first and shuddered in the sky as something shuddered in me, perhaps a sob. Then it vanished. I felt I continued to sink into that frightful, narrow, lonely space into which I had looked, leaning over the wooden parapet. But Father, standing at my shoulder, said:

"You will see: very soon elephants will come after their ivory and tortoises after your comb."

I smiled.

"They will come to take what by all rights belongs to them and which we took from them."

"I don't know, I don't know, this is a complicated problem. But they will come."

I knew he was right, and though he spoke to me then as with a child I did not protest.

Perhaps I should have told him I was now living in a deep well. Or asked him how and when his source had burst. But I did not ask. I feared he had no source or that his source would never help me.

(And how would I manage with that deaf, stupid old snake who could not hear my pipe?)

Night passed, and the moon like an hour hand moved along, rising and falling on the celestial dial strewn with stars that were more numerous the more I looked at them: they were stones, fire, lava, explosions, heat, steam, whirling, and silence.

Fyodor Dostoyevsky

WHITE NIGHTS

IT WAS A wonderful night, such a night as is only possible when we are young, dear reader. The sky was so starry, so bright that, looking at it, one could not help asking oneself whether ill-humored and capricious people could live under such a sky. That is a youthful question too, dear reader, very youthful, but may the Lord put it more frequently into your heart! . . . Speaking of capricious and

Novelist Fyodor Dostoyevsky is the author of numerous classics of Russian literature, including Crime and Punishment, The Brothers Karamazov *and* Notes from the Underground. *As a boy, he was sent to military school in St. Petersburg, where he eschewed engineering and turned to writing. His story "White Nights" is from 1918.*

ill-humored people, I cannot help recalling my moral condition all that day. From early morning I had been oppressed
by a strange despondency. It suddenly seemed to me that I
was lonely, that every one was forsaking me and going away
from me. Of course, any one is entitled to ask who "every
one" was. For through I had been living almost eight years in
Petersburg I had hardly an acquaintance. But what did I want
with acquaintances? I was acquainted with all Petersburg as it
was; that was why I felt as though they were all deserting me
when all Petersburg packed up and went to its summer villa.
I felt afraid of being alone, and for three whole days I wandered about the town in profound dejection, not knowing
what to do with myself. Whether I walked in the Nevsky,
went to the Gardens or sauntered on the embankment, there
was not one face of those I had been accustomed to meet at
the same time and place all the year. They, of course, do not
know me, but I know them. I know them intimately, I have
almost made a study of their faces, and am delighted when
they are gay, and downcast when they are under a cloud. I
have almost struck up a friendship with one old man whom I

meet every blessed day, at the same hour in Fontanka. Such a grave, pensive countenance; he is always whispering to himself and brandishing his left arm, while in his right hand he holds a long gnarled stick with a gold knob. He even notices me and takes a warm interest in me. If I happened not to be at a certain time in the same spot in Fontanka, I am certain he feels disappointed. That is how it is that we almost bow to each other, especially when we are both in good humor. The other day, when we had not seen each other for two days and met on the third, we were actually touching our hats, but realizing in time, dropped our hands and passed each other with a look of interest.

I know the houses too. As I walk along they seem to run forward in the streets to look out at me from every window, and almost to say: "Good-morning! How do you do? I am quite well, thank God, and I am to have a new storey in May," or, "How are you? I am being redecorated tomorrow"; or, "I was almost burnt down and had such a fright," and so on. I have my favorites among them, some are dear friends; one of them intends to be treated by the architect this summer. I shall go every day on purpose to see that the operation is not a failure. God forbid! But I shall never forget an incident with a very pretty little house of a light pink color. It was such a charming little brick house, it looked so hospitably at me, and so proudly at its ungainly neighbors, that my heart rejoiced whenever I happened to pass it. Suddenly last week I walked along the street, and when I looked at my friend I heard a plaintive, "They are painting me yellow!" The villains! The barbarians! They had spared nothing, neither columns, nor cornices, and my poor little friend was as yellow as a canary. It almost made me bilious. And to this day I have not had the courage to visit my poor disfigured friend, painted the color of the Celestial Empire.

So now you understand, reader, in what sense I am acquainted with all Petersburg.

I have mentioned already that I had felt worried for three whole days before I guessed the cause of my uneasiness. And I felt ill at ease in the street—this one had gone and that one had gone, and what had become of the other?—and at home I did not feel like myself either. For two evenings I was puzzling my brains to think what was amiss in my corner; why I felt so uncomfortable in it. And in perplexity I scanned my grimy green walls, my ceiling covered with a spider's web, the growth of which Matrona has so successfully encouraged. I looked over all my furniture, examined every chair, wondering whether the trouble lay there (for if one chair is not standing in the same position as it stood the day before, I am not myself). I looked at the window, but it was all in vain . . . I was not a bit better for it! I even bethought me to send for Matrona, and was giving her some fatherly admonitions in regard to the spider's web and sluttishness in general; but she simply stared at me in amazement and went away without saying a word, so that the spider's web is comfortably hanging in its place to this day. I only at last this morning realized what was wrong. Aie! Why, they are giving me the slip and making off to their summer villas! Forgive the triviality of the expression, but I am in no mood for fine language . . . for everything that had been in Petersburg had gone or was going away for the holidays; for every respectable gentleman of dignified appearance who took a cab was at once transformed, in my eyes, into a respectable head of a household who after his daily duties were over, was making his way to the bosom of his family, to the summer villa; for all the passersby had now quite a peculiar air which seemed to say to every one they met: "We are only here for the moment, gentlemen, and in another two hours we shall be going off to the summer villa." If a window opened after delicate fingers, white as snow, had tapped upon the pane, and the head of a pretty girl was thrust out, calling to a street-seller with pots of flowers—at once on the spot I fancied that those flowers were being bought not simply in order to enjoy the flowers and the spring in stuffy town lodgings, but because they would all be very soon moving into the country and could take the flowers with them. What is more, I made such progress in my new peculiar sort of investigation that I could distinguish correctly from the mere air of each in what summer villa he was living. The inhabitants of Kamenny and Aptekarsky Islands or of the Peterhof Road were marked by the studied elegance of their manner, their fashionable summer suits, and the fine carriages in which they drove to town. Visitors to Pargolovo and places further away impressed one at first sight by their reasonable and dignified air; the tripper to Krestovsky Island could be recognized by his look of irrepressible gaiety. If I chanced to meet a long procession of wagoners walking lazily with the reins in their hands beside wagons loaded with regular mountains of furniture, tables, chairs, ottomans and sofas and domestic utensils of all sorts, frequently with a decrepit cook sitting on the top of it all, guarding her master's property as though it were the apple of her eye; or if I saw boats heavily loaded with household goods crawling along the Neva or Fontanka to the Black River or the Islands— the wagons and the boats were multiplied tenfold, a hundredfold, in my eyes. I fancied that everything was astir and moving, everything was going in regular caravans to the summer villas. It seemed as though Petersburg threatened to become a wilderness, so that at last I felt ashamed, mortified and sad that I had nowhere to go for the holidays and no reason to go away. I was ready to go away with every wagon, to drive off with every gentleman of respectable appearance who took a cab; but no one—absolutely no

one—invited me; it seemed they had forgotten me, as
though really I were a stranger to them!

I took long walks, succeeding, as I usually did, in
quite forgetting where I was, when I suddenly found myself
at the city gates. Instantly I felt lighthearted, and I passed the
barrier and walked between cultivated fields and meadows,
unconscious of fatigue, and feeling only all over as though a
burden were falling off my soul. All the passersby gave me
such friendly looks that they seemed almost greeting me, they
all seemed so pleased at something. They were all smoking
cigars, every one of them. And I felt pleased as I never had
before. It was as though I had suddenly found myself in
Italy—so strong was the effect of nature upon a half-sick
townsman like me, almost stifling between city walls.

There is something inexpressibly touching in nature
round Petersburg, when at the approach of spring she puts
forth all her might, all the powers bestowed on her by
Heaven, when she breaks into leaf, decks herself out and
spangles herself with flowers. . . . Somehow I cannot help
being reminded of a frail, consumptive girl, at whom one

sometimes looks with compassion, sometimes with sympathetic love, whom sometimes one simply does not notice; though suddenly in one instant she becomes, as though by chance, inexplicably lovely and exquisite, and impressed and intoxicated, one cannot help asking oneself what power made those sad, pensive eyes flash with such fire? What summoned the blood to those pale, wan cheeks? What bathed with passion those soft features? What set that bosom heaving? What so suddenly called strength, life and beauty into the poor girl's face, making it gleam with such a smile, kindle with such bright, sparkling laughter? You look round, you seek for some one, you conjecture. . . . But the moment passes, and next day you meet, maybe, the same pensive and preoccupied look as before, the same pale face, the same meek and timid movements, and even signs of remorse, traces of a mortal anguish and regret for the fleeting distraction. . . . And you grieve that the momentary beauty has faded so soon never to return, that it flashed upon you so treacherously, so vainly, grieve because you had not even time to love her. . . .

And yet my night was better than my day! This was how it happened.

I came back to the town very late, and it had struck ten as I was going towards my lodgings. My way lay along the canal embankment, where at that hour you never meet a soul. It is true that I live in a very remote part of the town. I walked along singing, for when I am happy I am always humming to myself like every happy man who has no friend or acquaintance with whom to share his joy. Suddenly I had a most unexpected adventure.

Leaning on the canal railing stood a woman with her elbows on the rail, she was apparently looking with great attention at the muddy water of the canal. She was wearing a very charming yellow hat and a jaunty little black mantle. "She's a girl, and I am sure she is dark," I thought. She did not seem to hear my footsteps, and did not even stir when I passed by with bated breath and loudly throbbing heart.

"Strange," I thought; "she must be deeply absorbed in something," and all at once I stopped as though petrified. I heard a muffled sob. Yes! I was not mistaken, the girl was crying, and a minute later I heard sob after sob. Good Heavens! My heart sank. And timid as I was with women, yet this was such a moment! . . . I turned, took a step towards her, and should certainly have pronounced the word "Madam!" if I had not known that that exclamation has been uttered a thousand times in every Russian society novel. It was only that reflection stopped me. But while I was seeking for a word, the girl came to herself, looked round, started, cast down her eyes and slipped by me along the embankment. I at once followed her; but she, divining this, left the embankment, crossed the road and walked along the pavement. I dared not cross the street after her. My heart was fluttering like a captured bird. All at once a chance came to my aid.

Along the same side of the pavement there suddenly came into sight, not far from the girl, a gentleman in evening dress, of dignified years, though by no means of dignified carriage; he was staggering and cautiously leaning against the wall. The girl flew straight as an arrow, with the timid haste one sees in all girls who do not want any one to volunteer to accompany them home at night, and no doubt the staggering gentleman would not have pursued her, if my good luck had not prompted him.

Suddenly, without a word to any one, the gentleman set off and flew full speed in pursuit of my unknown lady. She was racing like the wind, but the staggering gentleman was overtaking—overtook her. The girl uttered a shriek, and . . . I bless my luck for the excellent knotted stick, which happened on that occasion to be in my right hand. In a flash I was on the other side of the street; in a flash the obtrusive gentleman had taken in the position, had grasped the irresistible argument, fallen back without a word, and only when we were very far away protested against my action in rather vigorous language. But his words hardly reached us.

"Give me your arm," I said to the girl. "And he won't dare to annoy us further."

She took my arm without a word, still trembling with excitement and terror. Oh, obtrusive gentleman! How I blessed you at that moment! I stole a glance at her, she was very charming and dark—I had guessed right.

On her black eyelashes there still glistened a tear—

from her recent terror or her former grief—I don't know. But there was already a gleam of a smile on her lips. She too stole a glance at me, faintly blushed and looked down.

"There, you see; why did you drive me away? If I had been here, nothing would have happened . . ."

"But I did not know you; I though that you too . . . "

"Why, do you know me now?"

"A little! Here, for instance, why are you trembling?"

"Oh, you are right at the first guess!" I answered, delighted that my girl had intelligence; that is never out of place in company with beauty. "Yes, from the first glance you have guessed the sort of man you have to do with. Precisely; I am shy with women, I am agitated, I don't deny it, as much so as you were a minute ago when that gentleman alarmed you. I am in some alarm now. It's like a dream, and I never guessed even in my sleep that I should ever talk with any woman."

"What? Really? . . ."

"Yes; if my arm trembles, it is because it has never been held by a pretty little hand like yours. I am a complete stranger to women; that is, I have never been used to them. You see, I am alone . . . I don't even know how to talk to them. Here, I don't know now whether I have said something silly to you! Tell me frankly; I assure you beforehand that I am not quick to take offense? . . ."

"No, nothing, nothing, quite the contrary. And if you insist on my speaking frankly, I will tell you that women like such timidity; and if you want to know more, I like it too, and I won't drive you away till I get home."

"You will make me," I said, breathless with delight, "lose my timidity, and then farewell to all my chances. . ."

"Chances! What chances—of what? That's not so nice."

"I beg your pardon, I am sorry, it was a slip of the tongue; but how can you expect one at such a moment to have no desire. . ."

"To be liked, eh?"

"Well, yes; but do, for goodness' sake, be kind. Think what I am! Here, I am twenty-six and I have never seen any one. How can I speak well, tactfully, and to the point? It will seem better to you when I have told you everything openly . . . I don't know how to be silent when my heart is speaking. Well, never mind. . . Believe me, not one woman, never, never! No acquaintance of any sort! And I do nothing but dream every day that at last I shall meet some one. Oh, if only you knew how often I have been in love in that way . . ."

"How? With whom? . . ."

"Why, with no one, with an ideal, with the one I dream of in my sleep. I make up regular romances in my dreams. Ah, you don't know me! It's true, of course, I have met two or three women, but what sort of women were they? There were all landladies, that . . . But I shall make you laugh if I tell you that I have several times thought of speaking, just simply speaking, to some aristocratic lady in the street, when she is alone, I need hardly say; speaking to her, of course, timidly, respectfully, passionately; telling her that I am perishing in solitude, begging her not to send me away; saying that I have no chance of making the acquaintance of any woman;

impressing upon her that it is a positive duty for a woman not to repulse so timid a prayer from such a luckless man as me. That, in fact, all I ask is, that she should say two or three sisterly words with sympathy, should not repulse me at first sight; should take me on trust and listen to what I say; should laugh at me if she likes, encourage me, say two words to me, only two words, even though we never meet again afterwards! . . . But you are laughing; however, that is why I am telling you . . . "

"Don't be vexed; I am only laughing at your being your own enemy, and if you had tried you would have succeeded, perhaps, even though it had been in the street; the simpler the better. . . . No kind-hearted woman, unless she were stupid or, still more, vexed about something at the moment, could bring herself to send you away without those two words which you ask for so timidly. . . . But what am I saying? Of course she would take you for a madman. I was judging by myself; I know a good deal about other people's lives."

"Oh, thank you," I cried; "you don't know what you have done for me now!"

"I am glad! I am glad! But tell me how did you find out that I was the sort of woman with whom . . . well, whom you think worthy . . . of attention and friendship . . . in fact, not a landlady as you say? What made you decide to come up to me?"

"What made me? . . . But you were alone; that gentle—man was too insolent; it's night. You must admit that it was a duty. . . ."

"No, no; I mean before, on the other side—you know you meant to come up to me."

"On the other side? Really I don't know how to answer; I am afraid to. . . . Do you know I have been happy today? I walked along singing; I went out into the country; I have never had such happy moments. You . . . perhaps it was my fancy . . . Forgive me for referring to it; I fancied you were crying, and I . . . could not bear to hear it . . . it made my heart ache. . . . Oh, my goodness! Surely I might be troubled about you? Surely there was no harm in feeling brotherly compassion for you. . . . I beg your pardon, I said compassion. . . . Well, in short, surely you would not be offended at my involuntary impulse to go up to you? . . ."

"Stop, that's enough, don't talk of it," said the girl, looking down, and pressing my hand. "It's my fault for having spoken of it; but I am glad I was not mistaken in you. . . . But here I am home; I must go down this turning, it's two steps from here. . . . Good-bye, thank you! . . ."

"Surely . . . surely you don't mean . . . that we shall never see each other again? . . . Surely this is not to be the end?"

"You see," said the girl, laughing, "at first you only wanted two words, and now . . . However, I won't say anything . . . perhaps we shall meet. . . ."

"I shall come here tomorrow," I said. "Oh, forgive me, I am already making demands. . . ."

"Yes, you are not very patient . . . you are almost insisting."

"Listen, listen!" I interrupted her. "Forgive me if I tell you something else. . . . I tell you what, I can't help coming here tomorrow, I am a dreamer; I have so little real life that I look upon such moments as this now, as so rare, that I cannot help going over such moments again in my dreams. I shall be dreaming of you all night, a whole week, a whole year. I shall certainly come here tomorrow, just here to this place, just at the same hour, and I shall be happy remembering today. This place is dear to me already. I have already two or three such places in Petersburg. I once shed tears over memories . . . like you . . . . Who knows, perhaps you were weeping ten minutes ago over some memory. . . . But, forgive me, I have forgotten myself again; perhaps you have once been particularly happy here. . . ."

"Very good," said the girl, "perhaps I will come here tomorrow, too, at ten o'clock. I see that I can't forbid you. . . . The fact is, I have to be here; don't imagine that I am making an appointment with you; I tell you beforehand that I have to be here on my own account. But . . . well, I tell you straight out, I don't mind if you do come. To begin with, something unpleasant might happen as it did today, but never mind that . . . In short, I should simply like to see you . . . to say two words to you. Only, mind, you must not think the worse of me now! Don't think I make appointments so lightly. . . . I shouldn't make it except that . . . But let that be my secret! Only a compact beforehand . . ."

"A compact! Speak, tell me, tell me all beforehand; I agree to anything, I am ready for anything," I cried delighted. "I answer for myself, I will be obedient, respectful . . . you know me...."

"It's just because I do know you that I ask you to come tomorrow," said the girl, laughing. "I know you perfectly. But mind you will come on the condition, in the first place (only be good, do what I ask—you see, I speak frankly), you won't fall in love with me. . . . That's impossible, I assure you. I am ready for friendship; here's my hand. . . . But you mustn't fall in love with me, I beg you!"

"I swear," I cried, gripping her hand. . . .

"Hush, don't swear, I know you are ready to flare up like gunpowder. Don't think ill of me for saying so. If only you knew.... I, too, have no one to whom I can say a word, whose advice I can ask. Of course, one does not look for an adviser in the street; but you are an exception. I know you as though we had been friends for twenty years.... You won't deceive me, will you? . . ."

"You will see . . . the only thing is, I don't know how I am going to survive the next twenty-four hours."

"Sleep soundly. Good-night, and remember that I have trusted you already. But you exclaimed so nicely just now, 'Surely one can't be held responsible for every feeling, even for brotherly sympathy!' Do you know, that was so nicely said, that the idea struck me at once, that I might confide in you?"

"For God's sake do; but about what? What is it?"

"Wait till tomorrow. Meanwhile, let that be a secret. So much the better for you; it will give it a faint flavor of romance. Perhaps I will tell you tomorrow, and perhaps not. . . . I will talk to you a little more beforehand; we will get to know each other better . . ."

"Oh yes, I will tell you all about myself tomorrow! But what has happened? It is as though a miracle had befallen me. My God, where am I? Come, tell me aren't you glad that you were not angry and did not drive me away at the first

moment, as any other woman would have done? In two minutes you have made me happy forever. Yes, happy; who
knows, perhaps you have reconciled me with myself, solved my
doubts! . . . Perhaps such moments come upon me . . . But
there I will tell you all about it tomorrow, you shall know
everything, everything. . . ."

"Very well, I consent; you shall begin . . ."

"Agreed."

"Good-bye till tomorrow!"

"Till tomorrow!"

And we parted. I walked about all night; I could not
make up my mind to go home. I was so happy. . . .
Tomorrow!

Tatyana Tolstaya

MOST BELOVED

AT NIGHT SPRING blows through Leningrad. River
wind, garden wind, and stone wind collide, whirl together
in a powerful rush, and race through the empty troughs
of the streets, shatter the glass of attic windows with a
peal and lift the damp, limp sleeves of laundry drying
between the rafters; the winds fling themselves flat on the
ground, soar up again and take off, speeding the scents of

Tatyana Tolstaya is the author of two collections of short stories, On
the Golden Porch *and the 1991 volume* Sleepwalker in a Fog,
*from which "Most Beloved" is taken. Tolstaya is a distant relative of
Leo Tolstoy and the granddaughter of Alexi Tolstoy.*

granite and budding leaves out to the night sea where, on a distant ship under a fleet sea star, a sleepless traveler crossing the night will raise his head, inhale the arriving air, and think: land.

But by early summer the city begins to wear on the soul. In the pale evening you stand at the window above the emptying street and watch the arc lamps come on quietly—one moment they're dead and silent, and then suddenly, like a sick, technological star, a rosy manganese point lights up, and it swells, spills, grows, and brightens until it shines full strength with a dead, lunar whiteness. Meanwhile, outside of town, the grasses have already quietly risen from the earth, and without a thought for us the trees rustle and the gardens change flowers. Somewhere out there are dusty white roads with tiny violets growing along their shoulders, the swish of summer stillness at the summit of century-old birches.

Somewhere out there our dacha is aging, collapsing on one side. The weight of February snows has crushed the roof, winter storms have toppled the double-horned chimney. The window frames are cracking and weakened diamonds of colored glass fall onto the ground, onto the brittle litter of two years' flowers, onto the dry muddle of spent stems; they fall with a faint chime no one will hear. There's no one to weed out the stinging nettle and goosefoot, sweep the pine needles from the rickety porch, no one to open the creaky, unpainted shutters.

There used to be Zhenechka for all this. Even now it seems she might be limping along the garden path, in her hand the first bouquet of dill, raised like a torch. Perhaps she actually is somewhere around here right now, only we can't see her. But the cemetery is definitely not the right place for her—for anyone else in the world, yes, but not for her. After all, she meant to live forever, until the seas dry up. It never even crossed her mind that she could stop living, and, truth be told, we too were certain of her immortality—as we were of our own, for that matter.

LONG, LONG AGO, on the far side of dreams, childhood reigned on earth, the winds slept quietly beyond the distant, dark blue woods, and Zhenechka was alive. . . . And now, from the herbarium of bygone days which grows with every year—green and motley days, dull and brightly colored ones—memory fondly extracts one and the same pressed leaf: the first morning at the dacha.

On the first morning at the dacha, the damp glassed-in veranda still swims in green, underwater shadow. The front door is open wide, cold creeps in from the garden; the pails are in place, empty and resonant, ready for a run to the lake, to the smooth, blinding lake, where the reflected world fell upside down in the early hours of the morning. The old pail gurgles, a distant echo gurgles. You ladle the deep, cold silence, the stilled, smooth surface, and sit for a while on a fallen tree.

Cars will soon start honking outside the gates of the dachas, summer folk will pour out of the automobiles, and, sighing and moaning, a taxi-truck will turn around in the narrow, wooded dead end of the road, scraping on the low branches of maples, breaking off the fragile flowering elder. It will give a gasp of blue smoke and fall quiet. In the returning silence the only sound will be the thunder of the truck's wood sidepanels dropping, and on its high platform strangers' belongings, crowded with an upturned Viennese chair, will be shamelessly revealed to the eye.

And one automobile will drive straight through the gates, and from the wide-flung door will emerge a firm, elderly hand gripping a walking stick, then a leg in a high-buttoned orthopedic shoe, then a small straw hat with a black ribbon, and finally smiling Zhenechka herself, who will straightaway cry out in a high voice: "Look at the lilacs!" and then, "My suitcases!" But the bored driver will already be standing with the canvas bags in both hands.

Zhenechka will hurry into the house, exclaiming loudly over the aromas of the garden; she'll push open the casements impatiently, and with both hands—strong like a sailor's—pull branches of lilac into the rooms, their cold, purple curls rustling with noisy importance. Then she'll hurry to the sideboard to see whether the winter mice have broken her favorite cup, and the cabinet will grudgingly open its swollen doors, behind which Zhenechka's treasure whiled away the January nights alone in the stale, empty depths, alone with a graying, forgotten cookie.

She will walk through the rooms, as yet unwarmed by the sun; she'll unpack, hand out presents crackling with paper, shake fruit fudge and sweet cakes from packets, cram the corners of the rooms with bouquets of wild flowers, hang our smiling photographs above her bed; then she'll clear the desk, and stack it with textbooks, dictionaries, and dictation books. Not a single idle day will she allow us; she'll sit us each down for at least an hour of lessons geared to our respective ages. "We are legion—you can't teach us all!" We'll wriggle and hop about in front of Zhenechka. "Yes, I can," she'll answer calmly, looking for the inkwell. "Take pity on yourself," someone will whine. "Like Pushkin says, we're disgusting, lazy—no curiosity. . . ." "All of you are going to grow up to be educated people." "We won't grow up! We're slaves to our stomachs! We're denizens of the dark kingdom! Take the books and burn them all!" "Never mind, we'll manage," says Zhenechka, and she'll seize us roughly and kiss us each harshly with a convulsive love we accept indulgently: All right, let her love us. Already she's dragging the first victim to her lesson, saying, as always, "I taught your mama, you know. Your grandmother and I were childhood friends. . . ." And on her chest, in the folds of her dress, her hearing aid begins to chirr like a nightingale—the hearing aid that for some reason never works quite right. Well, then, we're back to lessons again, exercises and dictations; once again, sitting in the creaky wicker armchair, propping her bad leg against the walking stick, Zhenechka, in her measured voice, will begin patiently turning us into educated people, and with the heedlessness of childhood, we will again start to bait her. We'll crawl into the room where the current captive languishes at the copybook; we'll crouch behind Zhenechka's armchair—her hunched linen back, her clean soap smell, the willow creak—and take advantage of her deafness to prompt the giggling victim with wrong or indecent or ridiculous answers, or pass notes with calls to rebel against the slave driver, until Zhenechka notices something's up and, all in a dither, banishes the spies.

And beyond the windows, beyond the tinted panes; a fresh, flowered stillness, warm shadows beneath the pines, and the midday lake filled with blue, glinting through the boughs, all covered with patches of sun, with fleet wedges of rippled brightness. . . . But here we are, locked indoors, the table covered in green blotting paper, the thumbtacks rusted over the winter, the ink stains bleeding an official-looking lilac rainbow. And everything Zhenechka says—is boring, correct, old. If only she'd go into the garden or go drink coffee! "Zhenechka, how much longer?" "Underline the subject with one line, the predicate with two. . . ." "Zhenechka, the summer will be over!" The willow armchair gives a heavy sigh, the blue eyes gaze with calm reproach, the patient voice says: "There's a time to sow and a time to reap. . . . Sluggards never make scholars. . . . Live and . . ."

Ohh, isn't there something she's dying to do?

The evening fades, the dust on the road grows

old, dogs bark far away. We lie in our beds on cool pil-
lows, listening to the sighs and purrs of the day winding
down, the whispers of doors, muffled laughter. From the
attic—lighter than shadow, quieter than dust—dreams
descend, surging in a transparent wave and confusing what
has been with what never was.

Knocking, squeaking, and rustling, groping
through the twilight of the house, Zhenechka makes her
way to our beds, settles in and takes up an unending story
about bygone years—about the children she taught and
loved, about the wind that scattered them throughout the
wide world: some disappeared, some grew up and forgot,
some returned to dust. Dreams swirl like a warm shadow;
from the invisible cloud of soap and mint only her voice
emerges, sympathetic and soft, then cooing and enrap-
tured, unhurried, like a blissful June day. Transparent
visions float in dozing waters: a boy surfaces, a faraway
dark-eyed, light-haired, antique boy, who long, long ago
lay just like this in a dizzyingly distant white bed and listened to the murmur, the gurgle, the rise and fall of

Zhenechka's voice—a boat rocking on waves of drowsiness. His eyes dropped and shut, his fingers relaxed, his speechless lips parted—for the dark-eyed boy was mute. That's why Zhenechka was asked to come: to pity, love, and care for him; to croon lullabies and babble fairy tales about dark forests, about the cat and the wolf, about the seven orphaned goats; and, as the boy fell asleep, his muteness mingled with the night's, and his bed set sail under the low vault of dreams.

ZHENECHKA HAD BEEN in our house from time immemorial, and through the darkness of infancy I can make out her blue gaze bent over me on the day when the good fairies customarily gather with gifts and greetings for the newborn. I don't know what gift she intended for me: amid the bounty of gifts called life, Zhenechka's own gift, humble and small, could easily have been lost, or maybe she had nothing to offer but herself, nothing but the steady glow of love and tranquility that emanated from her smooth, clear soul.

Once she gave one of us, one of her girls, a pretty box: luxurious, satin, full of light blue envelopes for love letters. Embarrassed, she threw back the top, so that its taut blue silk reins quivered; on the inner side, hidden from idle eyes, she had written in her clear schoolteacher's hand: "If you were to ask for advice, I would say only one thing: Don't wish to be the prettiest, wish to be the most beloved." And we did wish this. But nothing came of it, of course, no more than it did for Zhenechka herself.

Her mouth was not made for kissing. No. It was simply a dry, prim, pedagogical mouth, which with age acquired that particular array of surrounding wrinkles that unmistakably indicates honesty, goodness, and simplicity— all those tiresome, well-meant, inarguable truths that its owner hastens to share with you: The north is cold, the south is hot; May mornings are better than November fogs; sun, lilies of the valley, and golden curls are good; tornadoes, toads, and bald patches are bad. And roses— roses are the best thing on earth.

Zhenechka always stuck to her routine, of course. She exercised in the morning. In all seasons, she kept the window cracked open at night, and made a point of waking early—not because she liked gray, dank dawns, but because she could be useful in the mornings. The luxury of idleness was unknown to her, coquetry beyond her ken, playfulness alien, intrigue incomprehensible, that's the reason Hymen ran from her, not because he was the least bit scared off by her hearing aid or her orthopedic shoe. No, those trifles appeared later—after the war, after the bomb that exploded close to her, when Zhenechka was already over fifty. That wasn't the reason, of course. After all, even legless people can get married and have a family; it's the soul that counts. And her soul was—well, they don't come any simpler.

If our souls are usually constructed like a kind of dark labyrinth—so that any feeling running in at one end comes out the other all rumpled and disheveled, squinting in the bright light and most likely wanting to run back inside—then Zhenechka's soul was built rather like a smooth pipe, with none of those back streets, dead ends, secret places, or, God forbid, trick mirrors.

And the face matched the soul: simple blue eyes, a simple Russian nose. It would even have been quite a nice-looking face if it hadn't taken forever to get from the nose to the upper lip. Short, fluffy hair, a style called "smoke." Braids when she was young, of course.

She wore simple muslin dresses, undergarments that were clean and cheerless; in winter she put on a shabby quilted cotton coat that she called her "fur," and covered her head with a tall boyar's hat; summer or winter she never removed her amber beads, worn not for beauty's sake but for her health, because she believed some sort of electricity emanated from them.

She taught Russian her whole life, and—if you think about it—how could it have been otherwise?

GIVING PRESENTS WAS her favorite activity. Winters in our Leningrad apartment, at the core of my childhood, there would be a ring at the door, and—smiling, squinting, treading heavily on her orthopedic shoe, leaning on her staff—little boyar Zhenechka would enter in her cloth "fur," a real fur hat over her puffed hair, a fresh ruddiness on her middle-aged cheeks, in her hands a pastry box and other tiny, mysterious bundles.

We would all run out into the foyer; smiling silently, Zhenechka would hand over her things—the staff to the right, the tall hat to the left—and unbutton her heavy coat. Freed from its padding, the hearing aid on her chest filled with our cries and greetings, the smack of our kisses, shouts about how young she'd gotten and how well she looked. Having combed the fluffy smoke at the mirror and straightened the heavy amber beads, Zhenechka got down to passing out her gifts: for the grown-ups, useful, serious, books that got leafed through, set aside, and never picked up again; for us, tiny flasks of perfume, little notebooks, or surprising trifles miraculously preserved from the prerevolutionary times—statuettes, embroidered brooches, ancient cups with broken handles—treasures to take any little girl's breath away. Amazing how all these easily lost, perishable little things filtered down through the years. Time's meat grinder readily destroys big, solid, cumbersome objects—cabinets, pianos, people—while all manner of fragile odds and ends that appeared on God's earth to gibes and raised eyebrows—all those little porcelain dogs, miniature cups, minuscule vases, rings, drawings, snapshots, boxes, notes, knick-knacks, thingamajigs, and whatchamacallits—pass through unscathed. Zhenechka's tiny apartment somewhere on the edge of the city near the sea was crammed with all this marvelous junk, while her sisters—the three here and the fourth, who'd gone to live in Helsingfors, beyond the sea, beyond its sad, gray waters—had vanished like smoke. We were all she had left in the world.

Having handed everything out and received the happy squeals and kisses due her, Zhenechka picked up her pastries and marched off to the parlor to drink coffee.

The pastries, of course, were from Nord—the best. On her bad legs, Zhenechka had stood in a long line for them in that magical basement, that gathering place for all believers in sugary terrestrial bliss, where impatient ladies intent on instant happiness elbow their way over to the side gripping a pastry in tremulous fingers and— pressed by the crowd to the mirrored column, to their own agitated reflections—snort like eager fairy-tale stallions, their nostrils exhaling a double, swirling puff of sweet powder that slowly settles on their silver-fox collars.

Zhenechka would open the box wherein reposed the grand, monarchical pastries Napoleon and Alexander; beside them, like Dmitry the Pretender, the despised shortbread ring, that constant of railroad snack bars, had wormed its way in. No one would eat it, but to Zhenechka it, too, seemed wonderful—the ruddy embodiment of a sated, crumbly dream dreamt during the not-yet-forgotten hungry nights of the wartime blockade.

Until the pastries are gone, being with Zhenechka holds my interest, and then, alas, it's boring. She talks in detail about her health, the contents of a book she read, the flowers that grow so luxuriantly in summer at a friend's house near the Peri station (from the station walk straight ahead, turn left, then one more turn, and it's the second house) but don't grow at all in winter because of the fact that in the winter the ground is covered with snow, which falls from the sky, and thus unfortunately nothing can grow, but as soon spring comes and the days get longer and the nights shorter and the sun starts warming things and leaves appear on the trees, then, of course, the flowers will bloom again. . . .

I slip quietly out of the room and off to the kitchen; that's where real life is! Marfa, the housekeeper, is drinking tea with the lady who operates the elevator. Marfa is a tall, bald, cunning old peasant woman who was washed up at our door by the war; she knows absolutely everything better than everybody.

". . . So he says keep an eye on my suitcase, lady, will you? I'll be back, he says, in the wink of an eye. So she takes it from him. Right away he's up and gone. Well, he's gone for an hour, and he's gone for two, and now she has to go home. She's bone-tired of waiting. She figures she'll hand it over to the police, but she thinks, well, I'll just take a look-see. So she peeks inside." Marfa raises her eyebrows up high, pokes the sugar lumps with the tongs.

"Well?" says the elevator lady, alarmed.

"Well to you too. A fine how-de-do! She thought maybe there's valuables in there, or something. Opens it up—Heavenly Mother of God! . . . A head, with mustaches!"

"Chopped off?!"

"Right to here. Just a head, dreary, with mustaches. Some guy, not too old. And the head tells her: Shut the suitcase, he says, and don't stick your nose where it don't belong!"

"Oh my! The head says that?"

"Yes. Well, she's off and running for all she's worth. And the head yells after her: 'Shut the suitcase, you stupid fool, or you'll be in big trouble!' And he starts cussin' her something fierce."

"No!"

"These was a pack of thieves, deary. That's what

they was. They'd take him along in that suitcase, give him to someone in line to hold on to, and from inside there he hears everything—who's got bonds hidden where, or lengths of cloth."

"So that's what they do!"

Horrified, I ask:

"The head, who was it?"

"Who, who, what's it to you? You go play. . . . That what's-her-name of yours—she still here? The one with the beads?

Marfa doesn't like Zhenechka: she doesn't like her shabby coat, her beads, her nose. . . .

"What a nose—a regular hose! If I had me a horn like that, I'd toot it on holidays! Such a laaa-dy! The same old gab all the time—yackety, yackety yak . . ."

Marfa laughs, the elevator lady also laughs, politely, into her hand, and I laugh along with them, betraying poor unsuspecting Zhenechka, may she forgive me! But it's true, she does go on—yackety, yackety . . .

"And I heard another," Marfa starts.

But there's already a deep blue beyond the windows, and there are voices in the foyer—Zhenechka is getting ready to go home. Exhausted, everyone rushes to kiss her, a bit ashamed that they were so blatantly bored and Zhenechka, a pure soul, didn't notice anything amiss.

And someone walks her to the tram while the rest watch out the window: under softly falling snow, leaning on her staff, in her tall hat, Zhenechka slowly shuffles away, back to her lonely dwelling.

And the tram will rush past wastelands, snowdrifts, fences, past low brick factories that send a roaring appeal into the steely winter murk, past buildings decimated by the war. And somewhere at the edge of town, where the cold fields begin, a wizened amputee tumbles into the dim, clanking car, stretches out his accordion, and sings, "Oh, woe is me, a poor old cripple, I'm only half a man, they think; if you don't help, my cares will triple, for I still need to eat and drink," and warm, shame-ridden coppers fly into his filthy hat.

The snowflakes are thicker, the white shroud denser, the streetlamp sways, seeing off the small, lame figure, the snowstorm sweeps away the faint, barely visible footsteps.

BUT SHE WAS actually young once! Just think—the sky above was not a whit paler than it is now, and the very same velvety black butterflies fluttered above the splendid rose beds, and the whistle of the grass under Zhenechka's cloth shoes was just as silky when she walked down the drive, canvas suitcase in hand, to her first pupil, the mute, dark-eyed boy.

His parents were good-looking and rich, of course; they had an estate, and the estate had a greenhouse with peach trees, and young Evgeniya Ivanovna, who had just finished school with honors, was photographed among the peach blossoms—homely, smiling pleasantly, with two long, fluffy braids remarkable for the fact that they grew thicker and fluffier at the bottom. The picture faded to an iodine yellow, but Zhenechka's smile and the peach blossoms still showed, while her mute charge had bleached away entirely—all we could see was a bright patch nestled up against Zhenechka.

WHEN SHE CAME to that long-ago family, the boy could speak only his name: Buba. The rest of the world was engulfed in his silence, although he heard everything and loved everyone, and must have come to love Zhenechka especially, for he often sat close by her, gazed at her with his dark eyes, and stroked her face with his little palms.

It was enough to move a person to tears, and the rich parents wept, blowing their noses into lacy handkerchiefs, while the bearded family doctor, whom they paid exorbitant sums to examine Buba, gave his indulgent approval to the new governess, though he didn't find her pretty. But Zhenechka wasn't touched and she didn't weep. All business, she immediately established a daily routine and never deviated from it in all the years that she lived with her charge. After a while, to the amazement of the parents and the envy of the bearded doctor, the boy began to talk—quietly and slowly, glancing at serious, attentive Zhenechka, forgetting by morning the words that he had learned the night before, mixing up his letters and losing his way in the maelstrom of sentences, but, still and all, he did begin to talk, and could even draw some scribbles. The letter *izhitsa* came out best—the least used, most unnecessary letter in the Russian alphabet.

On Zhenechka's instructions the rich parents bought dozens of lotto games, and mornings she would wake to a knock at the door; the boy was already waiting for her, holding under his arm a rattling box full of little cardboard squares covered with elusive, difficult, slippery black words: ball, bird, hoopstick.

Once she took a vacation and paid a visit to her Petersburg sisters—she was not destined to see the fourth, the most beloved one, in far-off Helsingfors. Called back to the peach estate by an urgent telegram, she found the rich parents sobbing, the bearded doctor tranquilly triumphant, and the boy silent. The flimsy film of words had washed from his memory during Zhenechka's absence;

the enormous rumbling world, fearsome and noisy, had reared up in menace and crashed down on him in all its nameless inarticulateness, and only when Zhenechka hurriedly unpacked her canvas bag and retrieved the bright ball she'd bought him did the boy cry out in recognition, gasping: "Moon, moon!"

They wouldn't let Zhenechka go off again; now her Petersburg sisters had to come to her. But her favorite sister somehow couldn't manage to get away from Helsingfors for a visit. And she never did.

There was some fear that Zhenechka would marry and abandon the peach family—a needless fear: her youth fluttered by and departed without attracting anyone's attention. There must have been men Zhenechka liked, who appeared and disappeared in her life, just as, if you turn a kaleidoscope for a long time, a rare, yellow shard of glass will occasionally tumble free and bloom like a broken star. But not one of them asked more of Zhenechka than true, steady friendship; there was no one whose eyes misted over at the thought of Zhenechka, and no one who made a secret of his acquaintance with her—such a pure, respectable, ennobling acquaintance. Zhenechka is an extraordinarily good person, someone would say, and everyone would ardently take up the cry: Oh, yes, wonderful! Simply unique! So honest. And decent. Uncommonly conscientious. A crystal-pure soul!

THERE WAS ONE short, stunted, meager love in Zhenechka's life; there was someone who troubled Zhenechka's clear soul—perhaps for a week, perhaps for her whole life; we never asked. But whenever she told the story of how she lived and whom she taught before the war, one episode trembled plaintively through the years; there was one episode she always faltered over, and her high, calm voice would suddenly break for a moment, always on the very same phrase: "Good tea, Evgeniya Ivanovna. It's hot." That's what someone said to her at three o'clock on one prewar February afternoon, in a warm wooden building. At the time, Zhenechka was teaching Russian in a quiet sewing school, vegetating amid the apple trees and kitchen gardens somewhere on the outskirts of the city. Tearing themselves away from the subtleties of constructing "Undergarments, Women's Winter" and bolero jackets, uncounted generations of young seamstresses plunged into the refreshing, well-ordered streams of Russian grammar, only to forget forever the blur of Zhenechka's face after leaving their alma mater. They scattered around the world, loving, giving birth, stitching, pressing; they sang, saw husbands off to war, cried, grew old, and died. But, resolutely taught by Zhenechka, even on their conjugal beds they remembered the correct spelling of negative prefixes, and on their deathbeds, in a mortal swoon, they could, if necessary, have parsed a sentence.

Zhenechka traveled to the seamstresses through the black dawn by ice-cold tram; she ran, cold and ruddy, into the thoroughly heated wooden office and immediately looked about for the one she cherished: a rather gloomy, stoop-shouldered history teacher. He would walk toward her without noticing her and pass her by, and she dared not gaze after him. Her face burned, her hands trembled a little as she opened the workbooks, but he—he walked about the same building as she and thought his own thoughts. Such was the love that was her lot.

No one knew, and no one will ever know, what words she silently sent him while he stood by the window of the teachers' lounge and looked out at the snowy yard, where sparrows swayed like dark berries on branches. She probably yearned to say something honest, serious, and unremarkable, to make a modest request: Notice me, love me—but who says that sort of thing out loud? No one knew where he had been before, this man, nor where he went, but he must have come from somewhere. Dark-faced, taciturn—he'd been gassed in the first war, people said. He coughed dully in the wooden corridors, clutching his sunken chest in its soldier's shirt, and he smoked, smoked in the cold vestibule, where clumps of cotton batting stuck out of the insulated doors, where a feeble pink sun shattered against frosty purple stems on the frozen sill. He warmed his hands at the tile stove, smoked another cigarette, and left to lecture the seamstresses on history; the sound of his cough and his quiet, rather strained voice came from behind the tightly closed doors. Such was the man who pierced Zhenechka's heart, but neither of them said anything important to the other. And then who was Zhenechka to him? Just a good coworker. There was nothing between them except the mugs of tea that she poured for him in the teachers' lounge after lessons—trembling, her knees weak from her own foolhardiness. Madness, madness . . . It was no ordinary cup; it was a loving cup, adroitly disguised as a comradely one: Zhenechka poured tea for all the teachers, but she didn't give everyone so much sugar. A dark blue, chipped mug with a black border—that was all. And he drank it gratefully and nodded: "Good tea, Evgeniya Ivanovna. It's hot." And Zhenechka's love—a homely, barefoot orphan—danced for joy.

That was it, and there was nothing more at all, and soon he disappeared, and there was no one to ask.

FAR OUTSIDE THE city, beyond the wasteland of the outskirts, beyond the weedy alder copses, off the big roads, amid the pine forests and glades of fireweed, abandoned, surrounded by overgrown lilac, the dacha quietly ages. The lock is rusting, the porch rots, thistle has strangled the flower beds, and prickly raspberry edges away from the fence and across the garden, timidly at first, then ever more boldly, twining into the nettle to form a burning hedge.

At night the wind rises and flies over the blustery, deserted lake; collecting a misty dust and the hum of uninhabited expanses, it tears an iron sheet from the roof, rumbles it about, and flings it into the garden. The wind-bent grass whistles, wild berries and the seeds of wild plants scatter on the humid night earth, sowing a gloomy harvest of dragon's teeth. And we thought Zhenechka was immortal.

We didn't listen to the end of her stories, and now no one will ever know what happened to the mute boy; we threw out unread the books she gave us; we promised to come visit her in her Leningrad apartment but we didn't mean it; and the older we grew the more excuses we found to avoid her cold, lonely home. And when we finally did come, how she rushed to and fro with joy, how she clutched us—already grown a head taller than she— with small, dry hands, how she flung herself from the table to the stove, where an apple pie was already well under way, how hurriedly she straightened a festive tablecloth on the round table, anchoring it firmly with a vase of autumn roses! And how hastily she smoothed out the high bed's worn silk coverlet, pale, like the fluid, frayed petal of an enormous rose abandoned by August and possessed by a dusty, indoor spirit, a coverlet so light it couldn't be thrown over the bed with one broad flap; rumpling in a slow glide, slack and indifferent, it descended unevenly, riding handfuls of stale household air as it fell and shuddering long after it landed, stirred by the thin streams of a warm draft, by the rumble of trucks outside. And, having eaten her pie, we would depart feeling awkward and relieved, and we would relish the autumn air, and laugh at everything, looking all around us eagerly for the arrival of love, which we expected any minute now—long, true love, everlasting and unique—while the love that leaned against the windowpane above and watched us go was too simple and mundane for us. But Zhenechka, thank God, didn't realize that. And she fervently awaited the new summer, awaited her rendezvous with the old dacha, with the new flowers, and with us, her beloved ones.

AND SUMMER CAME.

The era of cooks passed. Fed up, Marfa left, taking away in her trunk the little capital she'd accumulated from milk bottle deposits; the silver fox furs rotted in the storerooms, the factory fences fell apart, and Leningrad gardens turned crimson with wild roses. The school years were coming to an end, the examinations loomed ahead, and energetic Zhenechka prepared for a decisive summer of work. But all this voluntary service—drumming Russian grammar into the heads of ungrateful, sarcastic lazybones day after day; clearing the jungles of dense, stubborn, wily

ignorance; planting the cleared terrain with shapely gram-
matical trees, their spreading branches sibilant with the
fuzzy suffixes of Russian participles; trimming away dry
knots; grafting flowering branches into place and gathering
the fallen fruit—all this toil was apparently not enough
for her. The uneasiness of the eternal cultivator drove her
into the garden, once as untended and wild as the heads of
her pupils. We would urge her to stretch out in the chaise
lounge in the sun: What could be better for an old person—just cover your head with burdock leaves and doze
till dinnertime. But instead it was we who collapsed in the
chaise lounge, languid from sun and adolescence, while
Zhenechka tied a kerchief on her head and marched into
the overgrowth with shears and a rake. Who had the time
to notice that in place of molehills and mountains of
stinging nettle, swaying flowers rose in a gentle froth. In
her hands flowers seem to soar: ornate pink hydrangeas
like bombs ready to burst into red, or else blue ones like a
mousse of whisked sky tinged with smoky thunderheads;
thick peonies of dark, swooning velvet; and some frizzy,

nameless trifle that was splashed all about like a quivering white rain. Only her beloved roses did poorly, no matter how hard she tried. We knew that Zhenechka dreamed of a genuine red rose, pure and deep like the sound of a cello; but either the meager northern warmth held them back, or the earth in our garden rejected the timid roots—the roses grew small, waifish, consumptive.

ZHENECHKA WOULD COME onto the veranda greatly distressed, and casting an alarmed look at us, she'd say, "Worms are eating the roses." "Give 'em the old one-two," we answered, bored. "Make an example of them." "Cut off their quarterly bonus."

But she was afraid of them—of flower worms, and rain worms, and especially of mushroom worms; it was difficult to slip a basket of mushrooms past her watchful eye. Arrest, inspection, and destruction threatened our booty, so we had to hand the basket straight through the low kitchen window while someone stood watch. Hastily dashing icy well water over the slippery, jumping, liplike brown boletuses stuck with leaves, or the pale, wide russulas that crumbled like shortbread and squeaked in our hands, we would throw them back into the noisily boiling pot, using a straining spoon to hold back the mushrooms crawling over the rim and to skim off the turbid foam full of dead, floating worms. At the clunk of Zhenechka's orthopedic shoe we would work faster, bustling and giggling, and by the time she ceremoniously entered the kitchen, pushing open the door with a royal gesture, the burbling broth already shone with a dark transparent purity.

"No worms?" she would ask, grave and anxious. "No, no, Zhenechka, perfectly wonderful mushrooms each and every one!" And she would calm down, never dreaming that we could possibly fib, while behind her back, wild with adolescent laughter, someone would wipe the straining spoon clean of the dried gray foam teeming with white corpses.

And everyone else would look away in embarrassment, as if we'd deceived a child.

. . . AUGUST APPROACHES, EVENING descends; the dark forest stands with its back to us, facing the sunset, and watches the liquid crimson islands burn out in orange seas high overhead. The first star is out. The night damp gathers. Women sitting on porches pull the hems of their skirts over their knees, speak more softly, raise their dark faces to the heavenly stillness. A black tomcat steps noiselessly out of the black grass, places a black mouse on the stoop. Soon the last heavenly island will be extinguished, darkness will move in from the east, the lake will speak in heavy, muffled waves; the wild lake wind will billow, straighten out, and moan, tearing off into dark, unpeopled expanses to bend bushes, fell ripe seeds, drive nameless, prickly orbs through cooling clover valleys and through untrodden copses; with a drone, it will ascend to the agitated sky in order to blow away the first wisps of feeble, ephemeral stars as they slip into the abyss. Soon it will be time to get up, sigh, shake off specters, walk across the old boards; cups will clink, gas burners will flare like blue asters, the evening tea will trill.

Refrigerators will clank open, and the women, back from the stars, will stare mindlessly into their rumbling, dimly lit interiors, slowly recognizing the contours of terrestrial cutlets or dense, frozen cottage cheese.

Zhenechka, quietly aging, goes through the house, opens the kitchen drawers, whisks some sort of rag about, and steps out onto the silenced porch, holding her breath so as not to frighten the stillness. She puts her hands on my shoulders—dry old hands, chilled to the marrow—and I suddenly feel how small and light she is, how easily the night wind could carry her away to the dark, clamoring distances.

A lengthy, tranquil moment sets in, one of those moments when superstition says an angel is passing over, and Zhenechka begins, "Now, I remember . . . ," but we've all come to, started talking, and stood up; the porch clatters under our feet, and Zhenechka rushes to tell us the rest, but it's too late, the angel has come and gone in a gust of wind that covers her words. I see her lips moving, her naive, loving gaze reach out; the wind grabs Zhenechka, the years spill from the sky like stars and fall onto the greedy earth where they grow like thistle, goosefoot, and couch grass; the grasses rise higher, close in; the old house chokes and dies, footsteps are erased, paths are lost, and oblivion blossoms everywhere.

AN OLD PERSON is like an apple tree in November: Everything in him is falling asleep. In anticipation of night the sap stops flowing, the insensitive roots grow chill and turn to ice, while slowly, slowly the split branch of the dusty Milky Way spins overhead. With its head leaning back, its dry stumps stretched to the frost-furred stars, the obedient, perishable creature waits, submerged in somnolence, expecting neither resurrection nor spring, waits for the dull, speechless swell of time to roll over it, carrying everything along.

Time passed, and we became adults. Busy with our urgent affairs and our friends, our books, and our children, we brushed Zhenechka's life aside; it was harder and harder for her to leave her house, and she would phone to relate things that interested no one.

For a minute or two, I listen to her slow voice, then lay the receiver softly on the telephone table and run off: in the kitchen pots are boiling, hot oil is shooting from the skillet; in the dining room there's lively conversation, laughter, and news, and they're calling me to share it all. The doorbell rings, a frozen, rosy crowd enters in raucous fur coats, there's the clatter of skis, the thud of feet, the floors shake, the windowpanes shake, and beyond the windowpanes the frosty trees shake, bathed in a dusky winter gold.

Zhenechka's voice lies cozily on the tablecloth, unhurriedly telling the telephone book, ashtray, and apple core about its joys and worries. Complaining and marveling, admiring and wondering, her soul flows from the telephone receiver holes in an even stream, spills over the tablecloth, evaporates like smoke, dances like dust in the last rays of the sun.

"Why is the receiver off the hook?" someone asks. I grab the phone with barely wiped wet fingers and shout: "Yes, Zhenechka! Of course, Zhenechka!" and rush away again. Her hearing aid sings and chirps; she doesn't notice a thing.

"Well, what's she saying?" asks a passing member of the household.

"Let me listen. . . . Something about some Sofia Sergeevna who went to the sanatorium last summer and the roses they had there. . . . She says the roses were red and their leaves were green . . . in the sky was the sun . . . but at night the moon . . . and the sea was full of water . . . people swam, and got out of the water . . . and dressed in dry clothes and the wet clothes dried out . . . oh, and she asks how we are. Fine, Zhenechka! I said, we're fine, Zhenechka! Just fi-ine! Yes! I'll tell them! I'll tell them!"

We were all she had left in the world.

But there came a day in the middle of winter when—shaken to the depths of her soul, armed with a cracked walking staff, the remains of her boyar hat pulled low—Zhenechka appeared on the threshold with a long blue envelope in her hands.

Words buzzed and fluttered in the envelope, telling her that she was not alone in this world; that quite close by—just a stone's throw away, beyond the cold gulf, beyond the arc of green ice and the swishing pines, in the snow-covered city of Helsinki (formerly Helsingfors), in an A-frame house, around a cheerful fireplace—there lived the offspring of Zhenechka's long-lost favorite sister; that these offspring were waiting, couldn't wait for dear Aunt Eugénie to enter under the peaked roof, into their hospitable half-Finnish embraces, and to lay cellophane-wrapped flowers on the grave of her dear sister, who rests in a neat Finnish cemetery.

We saw Zhenechka off at the station. She was flustered and embarrassed, like Cinderella stepping into the pumpkin carriage drawn by mice; she clutched her canvas suitcase with her toothbrush and a change of underclothes inside it. We had seen these undergarments at the dacha, on the lakeshore at dawn, when Zhenechka did the hygienic exercises suitable for her age. The shifts consisted of rectangular, sackcloth panels, meticulously joined with a solid, eternal seam; these severe, soldierly items knew neither darts, nor flounces, nor any other tailor's mischief—they were just sturdy panels, like the white pages of a story about an honest, hardworking life, usefully lived.

A month later we went to meet her at the same station, ran the entire length of the train and couldn't find her. From one car emerged an impressive old lady with eyebrows black like a fallen angel's and thickly blushed cheeks, dressed in fluffy furs and a dignified hat. The porter carried her scented suitcases. Someone recognized Zhenechka by her orthopedic shoe.

"Well?" we asked.

"They've got everything over there," she said. And, overcome, she nearly fainted.

We took her home and made her tea.

After that, Zhenechka went to Finland every spring. And then each summer—shining and crazed, happy and youthful, she grew unheard-of flowers from Finnish seeds in the fragrant, revitalized garden of our dacha. Zhenechka's lacy underwear, celestial and lemon-colored, hung on a line above the flowers, and in her room incredible objects were heaped on her shelf: perfumes, lipsticks, nail polish. And the roses—red roses which had behaved capriciously for many years—suddenly flourished under Zhenechka's hands, shooting out new buds in swift succession. The Finnish fertilizer must have helped.

Zhenechka would catch us at the front door or in the garden, and excitedly thrust photographs at us for the umpteenth time: Zhenechka on a Finnish sofa in the living room, Zhenechka with her great-nephew—her new, adored pupil—clinging poignantly to her hand (what's his name again, Zhenechka? Koko or Pupu?), Zhenechka in the dining room at dinner: lettuce leaves and a couple of green weeds.

"They're very thrifty. And they follow a strict diet."

We looked at Zhenechka's belatedly blackened eyebrows and yawned, listening as she sang her hymns to the untold riches of the fish stores.

"But Zhenechka, do they have sprats in tomato sauce?"

"No, now I don't think I saw any sprats."

"Well, there you are. How about Wave fish paste?"

"I don't think so."

"Well, then! They're way behind us! Just look, our shelves are filled with them!"

And earnest Zhenechka did her best to argue and persuade.

"And where did you go while you were there?"

"Oh, I stayed at home. I took care of my great-nephew."

"And them?"

"They went to the Azores. They'd already bought the tickets," she said in justification.

So while the relatives lolled about on ocean beaches, the infatuated Zhenechka watered, weeded, and coddled her new sapling with the stubbornness of an insane gardener; she drew the barbarian alphabet on blue paper, so that the boy could meet his suntanned parents with a Russian poem or unpronounceable greeting. On her return to Leningrad, she took to writing postcards, choosing the prettiest: bouquets, golden Petersburg bridges, and the statue of the Bronze Horseman (her relatives mistook Peter the Great on his horse for the anarchist Kropotkin). And new love, which never comes too late, thundered and raged and cascaded over her from head to toe.

And we believed that Zhenechka was immortal, that youth can return, that a candle once lit will never go out, and that virtue, whatever we might think of it, will eventually be rewarded.

WE'LL CHOOSE A day, lock the doors behind us, descend the cold staircase, go out into the stuffy morning city, and leave for the dacha. Out there, pink grass sways and rustles in the warm wind, pine needles cover the old porch; with a slight shush there passes through the emptied, abandoned house the shadow of a shadow of she who once lived, simple as a leaf, clear as light, still as morning water: she who once naively desired to be the most beloved.

We'll step off the train onto the bare cement platform, walk under the aspen hum of the wires and on—through marsh and thicket, across hills and copses—to where the empty house sleeps beyond the glades of overgrown fireweed, where lilac has gone wild, where a cow taps his beak along the porch, where mice say to one another: "Let's live here for a while."

We made through the grass, parting the dense overgrowth with our hands like swimmers; we find the long-forgotten keys and look around, stretching arms numb from the weight of the bags. It's a damp, lushly blooming northern June. The old, crooked dacha sinks into the grass like a half-drowned boat. Lilac darkens the rooms, pines have crushed the veranda's fragile breast. The brittle fifes of bedstraw have opened their white umbrellas; disturbed, a mysterious young bird cries loudly; and tiny veronica blossoms litter every sunny clump of dry earth with dark blue.

There are no roads or paths in the ocean of grass yet, the flowers are not yet crushed, only a slight corridor can be discerned where we walked from the gates to the porch. It's a shame to break the dense, stiff clusters of lilac—a blue, snowy shadow lies on them as on a new-fallen, sparkling crust of ice. It's a shame to trample the quiet, thick grass forests.

We drink tea on the veranda. Let's spend the night. Why don't we ever come here? We could live here! But it's a long way to lug supplies. We should weed out the nettle. Plant some flowers. Repair the porch. Prop it up somehow. The words fall into the stillness, the impatient lilac has burst through the open windows and sways as it listens to our empty promises, our impossible projects, our rosy dreams fading in an instant: it's not true, no one will come, there is no one to come, she's gone, she's a shadow, and the night wind will blow away her dilapidated dwelling.

ONCE AGAIN ZHENECHKA packed her bags to go visit her Finnish relatives: for the baby an ABC book, for the nephews something stronger. She was only waiting for the letter, and it arrived. The relatives came straight to the point—they couldn't invite dear Eugénie to visit them anymore. She would understand, of course; after all, she had reached such a venerable age that what had happened to their neighbors' Aunt Nika could happen to her any minute. And enclosed was a photograph of this aunt in her coffin, all dressed up and motionless, surrounded by Russian Orthodox lace and Finnish bouquets. Look how badly Aunt Nika behaved; if dear Eugénie were to do the same thing during her visit there might be complications, trouble, misunderstandings . . . and who would pay for it all? Had dear Eugénie considered this? And she needn't write anymore, why strain her eyes—and she might get a cramp in her hand!

Zhenechka stood and stared at the photograph of an unknown old lady in a neat coffin, a graphic reproach to Zhenechka's lack of foresight. And the nightingale that had sung songs on her chest for many years grew deaf and shut its eyes tight. And fate, like a black wind flying into an open window, turned, stuck out its tongue, and shouted,

"Just try and be most beloved!" and with a deafening cackle snuffed the candle out.

. . . A light Karelian night. There's neither darkness nor crimson dawn: an endless white dusk. All the colors have drained away; the grainy half-moon seems a cloudy brushstroke in the luminous heights; gray garden shadows and crevasses of clotted twilight crawl along the earth; between the tree trunks in the distance, the flat lake glimmers in lackluster coves. A mosquito whines, eyes close. There's a rustling in the gray grass, the creak of cracked shutters. Overnight yet another colored pane will fall from the veranda, overnight the grasses will rise still higher, the path we walked in the morning will be swallowed up and our footsteps will vanish; fresh mold will bloom on the front porch, a spider will spin the keyhole shut, and the house will fall asleep for another hundred years—from the underground passages where the Mouse King roams, to the high attic vaults from which the fleshless steeds of our dreams take flight.

Prince Youssoupoff

THE DEATH OF RASPUTIN

By ELEVEN O'CLOCK everything was ready.

The samovar stood on the table, with various cakes and sweetmeats for which Rasputin had a great liking. On one of the sideboards was a tray with wines and glasses.

I was still alone in the house as I cast an eye over the room and its arrangements.

Antique lanterns, with panes of varied colours, lit the room from above; the heavy dark-red curtains were

Prince Felix Youssoupoff was standing in the room when Rasputin was assassinated. His chilling account is recorded in the 1927 book,
Rasputin.

drawn. In the open fireplace a huge fire was burning; the logs crackled and threw out sparks on the stone hearth.

The room was almost underground, and was ordinarily of a rather gloomy aspect; but now, thanks to the lighting and furnishings, it was astonishingly cosy. Moreover, the stillness which reigned lent an air of mystery, a sort of detachment from the world. It seemed that whatever might happen here would be hidden from mortal eyes and buried for ever in the silence of these stone walls.

A bell rang. It told me of the arrival of the Grand Duke Dmitri Pavlovich and the rest of my associates.

I went to meet them. They looked confident and in good spirits, but they all talked rather loudly and seemed unnaturally gay, as if their nerves were on edge.

We passed into the dining-room. The arrangement of it greatly impressed my friends, particularly the Grand Duke Dmitri Pavlovich, who had seen it the day before, when nothing was as yet ready.

They all stood in silence for a while, as they examined the scene of the approaching event.

I drew from the labyrinth cupboard a box containing poison, and took from the table a plate of cakes; there were six—three with chocolate, and three with almond icing.

Dr. Lazovert put on rubber gloves and took out the crystals of cyanide of potassium. He crushed them, and having removed the upper layers from the chocolate cakes, sprinkled each of them with a strong dose of poison, afterwards replacing the tops.

We followed his movements with strained attention. A tense silence reigned in the room.

All that now remained to be done was to shake some powdered crystals into the wine-glass. We decided to do this at the last possible moment, so that the poison might not lose strength by evaporation. The total amount of poison applied was enormous: the doctor assured us that the dose was many times stronger than would be required to cause death.

To make everything appear natural it was necessary that there should be a number of used cups on the table, as though people had just taken tea. I had explained to Rasputin that when we had visitors tea was served in the lower dining-room, and that after the others had gone upstairs I sometimes remained below, reading.

We slightly disarranged the table and the room, drawing back the chairs, and pouring a little tea into the cups. I further arranged with the Grand Duke Dmitri Pavlovich, Sukhotin, and Purishkevich, that within ten minutes of my departure they should go upstairs to my study and turn on the gramophone, selecting the most cheerful records they could find. My object was to keep Rasputin in good humour, and to clear his mind of all suspicion. For I could not entirely rid myself of the fear that the underground situation of the rooms might put him on his guard.

When all these preparations had been completed, Dr. Lazovert and I left the room. He changed into chauffeur's clothes and went to start the car which was standing at the side entrance in the courtyard, while I put on a voluminous fur cloak and a fur cap with ear-pieces, which served to conceal my face.

We got into the car and drove off.

My head was a whirl of thoughts. I was sustained by my hopes for the future. During those few short minutes of my last drive to Rasputin's I lived through a whole life of emotions.

The car stopped outside No. 64, Gorokhovaya Street.

On entering the courtyard I was at once challenged by the *dvornik*.

"Whom do you want?"

On learning that I wanted to see Grigori Efimovich he was unwilling to let me pass, and insisted that I should give my name and explain why I was calling at so late an hour.

I replied that Grigori Efimovich himself had asked me to come at this particular hour and to go up to him by the back staircase. The *dvornik* looked me over with distrust, but nevertheless allowed me to pass.

The staircase was in darkness, and I had to feel my way. I had not even any matches with me. With great difficulty I at last succeeded in finding the entrance to Rasputin's flat.

I rang, and in reply heard his voice from behind the closed door: "Who's there?"

I shuddered.

"Grigori Efimovich, it is I. I've come to fetch you," I answered.

I heard him moving and bustling about. The door was chained and bolted, and I felt uneasy as the chain clanged and the heavy bolt grated at his touch.

He led the way, and I went into the kitchen.

It was in darkness, and I felt that someone was watching me from the adjoining room. Instinctively I turned up my collar and pulled down my cap.

"What are you muffling yourself up like that for?" asked Rasputin.

"Why, didn't we decide that no one should know about tonight?" I replied.

"True, true. I haven't told anybody here, and I've sent off all the *tainiki.* Come on; I'll get ready."

We went into his bedroom, which was particularly lit by a lamp in the corner, in front of the ikons. Rasputin applied a match to a candle. I noticed that the bed was disarranged—he had evidently just been resting. His fur coat and beaver hat were in readiness. On the floor was a pair of snow boots.

He was dressed in a white silk blouse embroidered with cornflowers and girded with a thick raspberry-coloured cord with large tassels, wide trousers of black velvet, and long boots, brand-new. Even his hair and beard were carefully combed and smoothed. As he drew nearer to me I felt a strong smell of cheap soap. He had obviously paid special attention to his toilet that day; certainly. I had never before seen him so clean and tidy.

"Well," Grigori Efimovich, isn't it time we were off? It's already nearly one o'clock."

"Shall we go on to the gypsies? What d'you say?" he asked.

"I don't know—perhaps—" I answered.

"But there won't be anybody special at your place

tonight?" he said, with a note of uneasiness in his voice.

I calmed him down by telling him that he would meet no one whom he disliked, and that my mother was still in the Crimea.

"I don't like her, your mother. And she can't stand me, I know . . . she's a friend of 'Lizbeth.' They're both digging pits for me, and slandering me. . . . The Empress herself has told me time and again that they're my worst enemies. . . .

"And, what d'you think?" he added, unexpectedly. "Protopopov drove round here this evening, and made me promise that I'd stay at home during these next few days. 'They want to kill you,' he said. 'Evil-minded people are plotting against you.' Ah, well! Let 'em plot. They won't succeed—they haven't got a long enough reach.

"But what's the use of talking about it! Let's go!"

I picked up his coat from a chest and helped him into it.

"Money—I've forgotten my money," he said, in a fluster. He went to the chest, and opened it.

I moved nearer; and, looking into it, I saw a number of parcels wrapped in newspaper.

"Surely that isn't all money?" I asked.

"Of course it is—nothing but bank-notes; I got 'em today," he answered without hesitation.

"Who gave them to you?"

"Various kind people. I just fixed up a little affair, and out of gratitude they made a donation to the Church."

"I suppose there's a good deal of money there?"

"Why should I bother to count it? I haven't time. I'm not a banker! That's a job for Mitka Rubinstein; he's got pots of money. Besides, to tell you the truth, I can't count it. I just said to 'em. 'Bring fifty thousand, otherwise I shan't worry over you.' Well, and they sent it. Perhaps they've given more! How should I know?

"It'll make a nice little wedding present for my daughter," he continued. "She's going to be married soon, to an officer with four St. George's Crosses. He earned 'em, too. And there's a fat little job waiting for him. 'She' has promised to give her blessing."

"But, Grigori Efimovich, didn't you say that this money was a donation to the Church?"

"Well, what about that? There's nothing to be surprised at! Marriage is of God, isn't it? The Lord Himself gave His blessing at Cana, in Galilee. And as to the particular use to which this money is put, isn't it all the same to Him—to God?" replied Rasputin with a cunning leer.

I could not help being amused at the naïve insolence with which Rasputin played with the words of the Holy Scriptures.

He took some money from the chest, which he then carefully locked. He blew out the candle, and the room was again in semi-darkness—illuminated only by the lamp which burned fitfully before the ikon in the corner.

I was suddenly overwhelmed by a feeling of infinite pity for this man.

I felt disgusted and ashamed at the thought of the vile means and appalling deception with which I was luring him to my home. Here was my victim—standing before me, suspecting nothing, trusting me.

At that moment I was filled with the deepest contempt for myself; I asked myself how I could have decided to commit such a hideous crime; and I could not understand how it had happened.

He trusted me. . . . But what had become of his insight? What had happened to his instinct? It seemed as if fate had somehow clouded his reason, and blinded him to our intentions.

But then I saw, with amazing clearness, one scene after another from the life of Rasputin. All my qualms of conscience, all my remorse vanished, and gave place to a steadfast determination to complete the task which we had undertaken.

I hesitated no longer.

We walked towards the dark landing, and Rasputin closed the door behind him.

The lock again grated noisily, and a harsh, ominous echo rang down the deserted staircase. We were in total darkness.

I felt a vice-like grip on my arm.

"I'll show you the way," said Rasputin as he led me down. His grasp hurt me. I wanted to protest and shake it off; but I felt numb. . . . I do not remember anything that he said to me, or whether I replied. At that moment there was only one thing I desired: to get into the open air as soon as possible, to see as much light as possible, and not to feel the touch of that terrible hand.

As soon as we got downstairs my horror left me, and I again became cool and collected.

We got into the car and drove off.

I looked through the rear window to find out whether we were followed. Not a soul was to be seen in the darkness.

We proceeded by a circuitous route, and on reaching the Moika, we turned into the courtyard, and drew up at the side entrance.

ON ENTERING THE house I heard my friends' voices, and the sounds of a popular American song on the gramophone. Rasputin stopped to listen:

"What's this going on?—a party?"

"No; my wife has friends with her. They will go away soon, so for the time being let's go down to the dining-room and have some tea."

We went downstairs. Rasputin removed his fur coat and proceeded to scrutinise the room and furniture.

He was particularly interested in the labyrinth cupboard. He showed quite a childish delight in it, and returned to it again and again, opening and shutting the small doors and examining the interior. He refused at first to take either tea or wine.

"Does he suspect anything?" I wondered; but I there and then decided that in any case he should not leave the house alive.

We sat down to the table, and talked. We discussed mutual friends, the G——s and Vyrubova; and we touched with Tsarskoe Selo.

"Grigori Efimovich, why did Protopopov come to you? Is he in constant fear of a plot against you?" I asked.

"Yes, I'm a stumbling-block to a good many

people, because I'm always telling the truth. . . . Your aristocrats don't like the idea of a common *muzhik* wandering about the Palaces. It's all sheer envy and malice. But why should I be afraid of them? . . . they can't do any harm to me: I'm proof against evil designs. They've had more than one try, but the Lord laid their plans bare. Take Khvostov. He tried it on, but he was punished and dismissed. They daren't even touch me. They'd only get into trouble."

His words sounded ominous.

But nothing could now dismay me. During the whole of that conversation I had only one idea in my head: to make him drink wine out of those poisoned glasses, and to eat the poisoned cakes.

He exhausted his ordinary topics after a time, and asked for some tea.

I poured him out a cup, and pushed a plate of biscuits towards him. Why I offered him the biscuits which were not poisoned, I cannot explain.

It was only some time afterwards that I took the plate of poisoned cakes and passed them to him.

He declined them at first.

"Don't want 'em; they're too sweet," he said.

However, he soon took one, then a second. . . . Without moving a muscle I watched him take them and eat them, one after another.

The cyanide should have taken immediate effect; but to my utter amazement he continued to converse with me as if he were none the worse for them.

I then suggested that he should sample our Crimean wines.

Again he refused.

Time passed. I began to get impatient. I poured out two glasses, one for him, the other for myself. I placed his glass in front of him and began to drink out of my own, thinking that he would follow my example.

"Well, let me try it," said Rasputin, stretching out his hand for the wine. It was not poisoned.

Why I first gave him the wine in an unpoisoned glass I am also at a loss to explain.

He drank it with obvious pleasure, praised it, and

asked if we had much of it. On hearing that we had a whole cellarful, he showed great astonishment.

He became animated. "Now give me some Madeira," he said.

I got up to take another glass, but he protested:

"Pour it into this one."

"But that's impossible, Grigori Efimovich. You can't mix red wine with Madeira."

"Never mind; pour it out into this, I tell you."

I had to give way.

By an apparent accident, however, I soon managed to knock his glass to the floor, where it smashed.

I took advantage of this to pour wine into one of the glasses containing cyanide of potassium. Having once begun to drink, he made no further protest.

I stood in front of him and followed each movement he made, expecting every moment to be his last.

But he drank slowly, taking small sips at a time, just as if he had been a connoisseur.

His face did not change; but from time to time

he put his hand to his throat as if he found slight difficulty in swallowing. He got up and moved about the room, and when I asked him whether anything was the matter, "Oh, nothing much," he said, just an irritation in the throat.

There was a nerve-racking pause.

"That's very good Madeira. Give me some more," said Rasputin, holding out his glass.

The poison still had no effect. The *starets* continued to walk about the room.

I took no notice of the glass which he held out to me, but seized another poisoned one from the tray. I poured wine into it, and passed it to him.

He drained it; and still the poison had no effect.

There remained the third and last glass.

In despair I began to drink myself, hoping to induce him to drink more and more.

We sat opposite each other in silence.

He looked at me with a cunning smile. I seemed to hear him say:

"You see! It doesn't matter how you try; you can't do me any harm."

But all of a sudden, his expression changed into one of fiendish hatred. Never before had he inspired me with such horror.

I felt an indescribable loathing for him and was ready to throw myself upon him and throttle him.

I felt that he knew why I had brought him there, and what I intended to do to him. A mute and deadly conflict seemed to be taking place between us. I was aghast. Another moment and I should have gone under. I felt that confronted by those satanic eyes I was beginning to lose my self-control. A strange feeling of numbness took possession of me. My head reeled. . . . I saw nothing. . . . I do not know how long this lasted. . . .

Rasputin was still sitting in the same position. His head was bent, and he was supporting it with his hands. I could not see his eyes.

I regained my presence of mind and offered him some tea.

"Yes, give me a cup; I'm terribly thirsty," he said in a weak voice.

He raised his head. His eyes were dim, and he seemed to be avoiding my glance.

While I was pouring out tea, he got up and paced about the room. His eyes fell upon the guitar which happened to have been left in the room.

"Play something," he begged. "Play something cheerful. I love the way you sing."

It was difficult to comply at such a moment . . . and he was asking me to sing "something cheerful."

"I'm not in the mood," I said as I took up the guitar.

He sat and listened attentively at first; but as I continued, his head dropped towards the table. He seemed half-asleep.

The moment I stopped he opened his eyes and looked at me with a calm and sad expression in them.

"Sing another," he said.

I sang again.

My voice sounded strange in my ears.

Time passed. . . . The hands of the clock pointed to half-past two. This nightmare had lasted over two hours.

"What will happen if my nerves don't hold out?" I wondered.

Upstairs, too, patience had evidently become exhausted.

The sounds from that quarter became more pronounced, and I was afraid that my friends would come down.

"What's all that noise?" asked Rasputin, lifting his head.

"Probably it's the guests going away," I replied; "I'll go up and see."

As I entered the study, the Grand Duke Dmitri Pavlovich, Purishkevich, and Sukhotin rushed towards me with revolvers in their hands.

Questions showered on me.

"Well? It is done? It is all over?"

"The poison has had no effect," I said.

They gazed at me in mute astonishment.

"Impossible," exclaimed the Grand Duke. "The dose was amply sufficient."

"Did he take it all?" asked the others.

"Every bit of it," I answered.

We began to discuss what to do next, and decided that we would go downstairs together, and throw ourselves on Rasputin, and strangle him. We were already carefully making out way down the staircase, when I suddenly realised that by doing this we should ruin everything. The unexpected appearance of strangers would at once warn Rasputin of our intentions, and there was no telling how matters would end. It had to remembered that we were not dealing with an ordinary type of man.

I called my friends back into the study and told them of my apprehensions. With great difficulty I persuaded them to leave me to finish with Rasputin alone. For a long time they would not agree; they had qualms on my behalf.

But finally I took the Grand Duke's revolver and went down to the dining-room.

Rasputin was sitting at the table, just as I had left him. His head was sunken and he was breathing heavily.

I went quietly up to him and sat beside him. He took no notice of my approach.

A few minutes passed in silence, and then he slowly raised his head and looked at me. His eyes were dim; with a dull, lifeless expression in them.

"Are you feeling unwell?" I asked.

"Yes, my head is heavy, and my stomach is burning. Give me another glass—that will ease me."

I poured him out some Madeira; he drank it at a gulp, and at once revived and regained his good spirits.

I exchanged a few sentences with him and saw that he was perfectly conscious, and that his mind was working normally. All of a sudden he suggested that we should go to the gypsies. I refused, on the ground that it was too late.

"What does that matter! They're used to it! They sometimes wait up for me all night. I'm sometimes kept at Tsarskoe Selo on important business, or just talking about God . . . but afterwards I drive over to them in the car.

The body also has to have a rest sometimes . . . isn't that true? With God in thought, but with mankind in the flesh. That's the idea," said Rasputin with a significant wink.

A conversation of this kind was the very last thing which I could have expected from him at that moment.

Here I had been sitting all that time with a man who had swallowed an enormous dose of the most deadly poison; I had been watching every one of his movements in the expectation of a fatal issue; and now he was suggesting that we should go to the gypsies! But what amazed me most was that in spite of his instinctive knowledge and insight, he should now be so utterly unconscious of his approaching end.

How could his sharp eyes fail to observe that, clenched in my hand, behind my back, was a revolver which in an instant would be aimed at him?

As this thought flashed through my mind, I looked round for some reason or other, and my glance fell on the crystal crucifix. I rose and went up to it.

"What are you doing over there so long?" asked Rasputin.

"I love this cross; it's a very beautiful thing," I answered.

"Yes, it's a nice thing. Cost a lot of money, I'm sure. . . . How much did you pay for it?"

He came towards me, and without waiting for an answer he continued:

"But this is what takes my fancy most." And again he opened the labyrinth cupboard and began to examine it.

"Grigori Efimovich, you had better look at the crucifix, and say a prayer before it."

Rasputin looked at me in amazement, and with a trace of fear.

I saw a new and unfamiliar expression in his eyes, a touch of gentleness and submission. He came right up to me, looking me full in the face, and he seemed to read in my glance something which he was not expecting. I realised that the supreme moment was at hand.

"God give me strength to end it all," I thought,

and I slowly brought the revolver from behind my back. Rasputin was still standing motionless before me, his head turned to the right, and his eyes on the crucifix.

"Where shall I shoot?" I thought. "Through the temple or through the heart?"

A streak of lightning seemed to run through my body. I fired.

There was a roar, as from a wild beast, and Rasputin fell heavily backwards on the bear-skin rug.

I heard a noise on the staircase: my friends were hurrying to my aid. In their haste they caught against the main switch just outside the room, and I suddenly found myself in darkness.

Someone stumbled against me and called out in fright.

I did not move; I was afraid of stepping onto the body in the dark.

The light was switched on at last.

They all rushed towards Rasputin. . . .

He was lying on his back. His face twitched

now and then; his hands were convulsively clenched; his eyes were closed.

There was a small red spot on his light silk blouse.

We bent over him, and looked at him closely.

Some of those present wanted to fire at him again, but were restrained by fear of leaving unnecessary traces of blood.

In a few minutes Rasputin became quite still.

We examined the wound. The bullet had passed through the region of the heart. There could be no doubt about it; he was dead.

The Grand Duke Dmitri Pavlovich removed the body from the bearskin to the stone floor. We switched off the electric light, closed and locked the dining-room door, and went upstairs to my study.

We all felt elated, so convinced were we that the events of that night would deliver Russia from ruin and dishonour.

Anna Akhmatova

VERSES ABOUT PETERSBURG

I

ONCE MORE ST. Issac's wears robes
Of cast silver.
And frozen in fierce impatience
Stands the horse of Peter the Great.

A harsh and stifling wind

In one outburst, from 1912-1923, Russian poet Anna Akhmatova published over a dozen volumes of intimate, lovelorn verse. She didn't publish again until the sixties, when her work took on a decisively political tone, decrying the horrors of Stalinism. "Verses about Petersburg" is contained in her collected works.

Sweeps soot from the black chimneys. . .
Ah! His new capital
Displeases the sovereign.

2

My heart beats calmly, steadily,
What are the long years to me!
Under the Galernaya arch
Our shadows, for eternity.

Through lowered eyelids
I see, I see, you with me,
And held forever in your hand,
My unopened fan.

Because we were standing side by side
In that blissful miraculous moment,
The moment of the resurrection of the rose-colored moon
Over the Summer Garden—

I don't need the waiting
At some hateful window,
Or the agonizing meetings—
All my love is satisfied.

You are free, I am free,
Tomorrow will be better than yesterday—
Over the Neva's dark waters,
Under the cold smile
Of Emperor Peter.

I know, I know—the skis
Will crunch on snow again.
There's a ginger moon in the dark blue sky
And the meadow slopes so delightfully.

The palace's little windows glow,

Remote in the stillness.
There are neither paths nor roads,
Only dark ice holes.

Willow, tree of water nymphs,
Don't block my way!
Shelter the black daws in your snowy branches,
The black daws.

John Reed

TEN DAYS THAT SHOOK THE WORLD

THE PROVISIONAL GOVERNMENT is deposed.
The State Power has passed into the hands of the organ of
the Petrograd Soviet of Workers' and Soldiers' Deputies,
the Military Revolutionary Committee, which stands at the
head of the Petrograd proletariat and garrison.

The cause for which the people were fighting:
immediate proposal of a democratic peace, abolition of

After graduating from Harvard, John Reed became obsessed with social struggle. He traveled to Russia, where he became an ardent supporter of the Bolsheviks—so much so that Lenin penned the introduction to Reed's famous 1919 account of the Russian evolution, Ten Days That Shook the World. *This book was the basis for the 1980 film,* Reds.

landlord property-rights over the land, labor control over production, creation of a Soviet Government—that cause is securely achieved.

LONG LIVE THE REVOLUTION OF WORKMEN, SOLDIERS, AND PEASANTS!

Military Revolutionary Committee
Petrograd Soviet of Workers' and Soldiers' Deputies

A slant-eyed Mongolian-faced man who sat beside me, dressed in a goatskin of Caucasian cape, snapped, "Look out! Here the provocators always shoot from the windows!" We turned into Znamensky Square, dark and almost deserted, careened around Trubetskoy's brutal statue and swung down the wide Nevsky, three men standing up with rifles ready, peering at the windows. Behind us the street was alive with people running and stooping. We could no longer hear the cannon, and the nearer we drew to the Winter Palace end of the city the quieter and more deserted were the streets. The City Duma was all brightly lighted. Beyond that we made out a dark mass of people, and a line of sailors, who yelled furiously at us to stop. The machine slowed down, and we climbed out.

It was an astonishing scene. Just at the corner of the Ekaterina Canal, under an arc-light, a cordon of armed sailors was drawn across the Nevsky, blocking the way to a crowd of people in column of fours. There were about three or four hundred of them, men in frock coats, well-dressed women, officers—all sorts and conditions of people. Among them we recognized many of the delegates from the Congress, leaders of the Mensheviki and Socialist Revolutionaries; Avksentiev, the lean, red-bearded president of the Peasants' Soviets, Sarokin, Kerensky's spokesman, Khinchuk, Abramovich; and at the head white-bearded old Schreider, Mayor of Petrograd, and Prokopovich, Minister of Supplies in the Provisional Government, arrested that morning and released. I caught sight of Malkin, reporter for the *Russian Daily News*. "Going to die in the Winter Palace," he shouted cheerfully. The procession stood still, but from the front of it came loud argument. Schreider and Prokopovich were bellowing at the big sailor who seemed in command.

"We demand to pass!" they cried. "See, these comrades come from the Congress of Soviets! Look at their tickets! We are going to the Winter Palace!"

The sailor was plainly puzzled. He scratched his head with an enormous hand, frowning. "I have orders from the Committee not to let anybody go to the Winter Palace," he grumbled. "But I will send a comrade to telephone to Smolny. . . ."

"We insist upon passing! We are unarmed! We will march on whether you permit us or not! cried old Schreider, very much excited.

"I have orders—" repeated the sailor sullenly.

"Shoot us if you want to! We will pass! Forward!" came from all sides. "We are ready to die, if you have the heart to fire on Russians and comrades! We bare our breasts to your guns!"

"No," said the sailor, looking stubborn, "I can't allow you to pass."

"What will you do if we go forward? Will you shoot?"

"No, I'm not going to shoot people who haven't any guns. We won't shoot unarmed Russian people. . . ."

"We will go forward! What can you do?"

"We will do something!" replied the sailor, evidently at a loss. "We can't let you pass. We will do something."

"What will you do? What will you do?"

Another sailor came up, very much irritated. "We will spank you!" he cried energetically. "And if necessary we will shoot you too. Go home now, and leave us in peace!"

At this there was a great clamor of anger and resentment. Prokopovich had mounted some sort of box, and waving his umbrella, he made a speech:

"Comrades and citizens!" he said. "Force is being used against us! We cannot have our innocent blood upon the hands of these ignorant men! It is beneath our dignity to be shot down here in the streets by switchmen—" (What he meant by "switchmen" I never discovered.) "Let us return to the Duma and discuss the best means of saving the country and the Revolution!"

Whereupon, in dignified silence, the procession marched around and back up the Nevsky, always in column of fours. And taking advantage of the diversion we slipped past the guards and set off in the direction of the Winter Palace.

Here it was absolutely dark, and nothing moved but pickets of soldiers and Red Guards grimly intent. In front of the Kazan Cathedral a three-inch field-gun lay in the middle of the street, slewed sideways from the recoil of its last shot over the roofs. Soldiers were standing in every doorway talking in loud tones and peering down towards the Police Bridge. I heard one voice saying: "It is possible that we have done wrong. . . ." At the corners patrols stopped all passers-by—and the composition of these patrols was interesting, for in command of the regular troops was invariably a Red Guard. . . . The shooting had ceased.

Just as we came to the Morskaya somebody was shouting: "The *yunkers* have sent word that they want us to go and get them out!" Voices began to give commands, and in the thick gloom we made out a dark mass moving forward, silent but for the shuffle of feet and the clinking of arms. We fell in with the first ranks.

Like a black river, filling all the street, without song or cheer we poured through the Red Arch, where the man just ahead of me said in a low voice: "Look out, comrades! Don't trust them. They will fire, surely!" In the open we began to run, stooping low and bunching together, and jammed up suddenly behind the pedestal of the Alexander Column.

"How many of you did they kill?" I asked.

"I don't know. About ten. . . ."

After a few minutes huddling there, some hundreds of men, the Army seemed reassured and without any orders suddenly began again to flow forward. By this time, in the light that streamed out of all the Winter Palace windows, I could see that the first two or three hundred men were Red Guards, with only a few scattered soldiers. Over the barricade of fire-wood we clambered, and leaping down inside gave a triumphant shout as we stumbled on a heap of rifles thrown down by the *yunkers* who had stood there. On both sides of the main gateway the doors stood wide open, light streamed out, and from the huge pile came not the slightest sound.

Carried along by the eager wave of men we were swept into the right-hand entrance, opening into a great bare vaulted room, the cellar of the east wing, from which issued a maze of corridors and staircases. A number of huge packing cases stood about, and upon these the Red Guards and soldiers fell furiously, battering them open with the butts of their rifles, and pulling out carpets, curtains, linen, porcelain, plates, glass-ware. . . . One man went strutting around with a bronze clock perched on his shoulder; another found a plume of ostrich feathers, which he stuck in his hat. The looting was just beginning when somebody cried, "Comrades! Don't take anything. This is the property of the People!" Immediately twenty voices were crying, "Stop! Put everything back! Don't take anything! Property of the People!" Many hands dragged the spoilers down. Damask and tapestry were snatched from the arms of those who had them; two men took away the bronze clock. Roughly and hastily the things were crammed back in their cases, and self-appointed sentinels stood guard. It was all utterly spontaneous. Through corridors and up staircases the cry could be heard growing fainter and fainter in the distance, "Revolutionary discipline! Property of the People. . . ."

We crossed back over to the left entrance, in the west wing. There order was also being established. "Clear the Palace!" bawled a Red Guard, sticking his head through an inner door. "Come, comrades, let's show that we're not thieves and bandits. Everybody out of the Palace except the Commissars, until we get sentries posted."

Two Red Guards, a soldier and an officer, stood with revolvers in their hands. Another soldier sat at a table behind them, with pen and paper. Shouts of "All out! All out!" were heard far and near within, and the Army began to pour through the door, jostling, expostulating, arguing. As each man appeared he was seized by the self-appointed committee, who went through his pockets and looked under his coat. Everything that was plainly not his property was taken away, the man at the table noted it on his paper, and it was carried into a little room. The most amazing assortment of objects were thus confiscated; statuettes, bottles of ink, bed-spreads worked with the Imperial monogram, candles, a small oil painting, desk blotters, gold-handled swords, cakes of soap, clothes of every description, blankets. One Red Guard carried three rifles, two of which he had taken away from *yunkers;* another had four portfolios bulging with written documents. The culprits either sullenly surrendered or pleaded like children. All talking at once, the committee explained that stealing was not worthy of the people's champions; often those who had been caught turned around and began to help go through the rest of the comrades.

Yunkers came out in bunches of three or four. The committee seized upon them with an excess of zeal, accompanying the search with remarks like, "Ah, Provocators! Kornilovists! Counter-revolutionists! Murders of the People!" But there was no violence done, although the *yunkers* were terrified. They too had their pockets full of small plunder. It was carefully noted down by the scribe, and piled in the little room. . . The *yunkers* were disarmed. "Now, will you take up arms against the People any more?" demanded clamoring voices.

"No," answered the *yunkers,* one by one. Whereupon they were allowed to go free.

We asked if we might go inside. The committee was doubtful, but the Red Guard answered firmly that it was forbidden. "Who are you anyway? he asked. "How do I know that you are not all Kerenskys?" (There were five of us, two women.)

"*Pazhal'st', tovarishchi!* Way, Comrades!" A soldier and a Red Guard appeared in the door, waving the crowd aside, and other guards with fixed bayonets. After them followed single file half a dozen men in civilian dress— the members of the Provisional Government. First came Kishkin, his face drawn and pale, then Rutenberg, looking sullenly at the floor; Tereshchenko was next, glancing sharply around; he stared at us with cold fixity. . . . They passed in silence; the victorious insurrectionists crowded to see, but there were only a few angry mutterings. It was only later we learned how people in the street wanted to lynch them, and shots were fired—but the sailors brought them safely to Peter-Paul. . . .

In the meanwhile unrebuked we walked into the Palace. There was still a great deal of coming and going, of exploring new-found apartments in the vast edifice, or searching for hidden garrisons of *yunkers* which did not exist. We went upstairs and wandered through room after room. This part of the Palace had been entered also by other detachments from the side of the Neva. The paintings, statues, tapestries, and rugs of the great state apartments were unharmed; in the offices, however, every desk and cabinet had been ransacked, the papers scattered over the floor, and in the living-rooms beds had been stripped of their coverings and wardrobes wrenched open. The most highly prized loot was clothing, which the working people needed. In a room where furniture was stored we came upon two soldiers ripping the elaborate Spanish leather upholstery from chairs.

They explained it was to make boots with. . . .

The old Palace servants in their blue and red and gold uniforms stood nervously about, from force of habit repeating, "You can't go in there, *barin*! It is forbidden—" We penetrated at length to the gold and malachite chamber with crimson brocade hangings where the Ministers had been in session all that day and night, and where the *shveitzari* had betrayed them to the Red Guards. The long table covered with green baize was just as they had left it, under arrest. Before each seat was pen, ink, and paper; the papers were scribbled over with beginnings of plans of action, rough drafts of proclamations and manifestoes. Most of these were scratched out, as their futility became evident, and the rest of the sheet covered with absent-minded geometrical designs, as the writers sat despondently listening while Minister after Minister proposed chimerical schemes. I took one of these scribbled pages, in the handwriting of Konovalov, which read, "The Provisional Government appeals to all classes to support the Provisional Government—"

All this time, it must be remembered, although the Winter Palace was surrounded, the Government was in constant communication with the front and with provincial Russia. The Bolsheviki had captured the Ministry of War early in the morning, but they did not know of the military telegraph office in the attic, nor of the private telephone line connecting it with the Winter Palace. In that attack a young officer sat all day, pouring out over the country a flood of appeals and proclamations; and when he heard the palace had fallen, put on his hat and walked calmly out of the building. . . .

Interested as we were, for a considerable time we didn't notice a change in the attitude of the soldiers and Red Guards around us. As we strolled from room to room a small group followed us, until by the time we reached the great picture-gallery where we had spend the afternoon with the *yunkers,* about a hundred men surged in upon us. One giant of a soldier stood in our path, his face dark with sullen suspicion.

"Who are you?" he growled. "What are you doing

here?" The others massed slowly around, staring and beginning to mutter. "*Provocatori!*" I heard somebody say, "Looters!" I produced our passes from the Military Revolutionary Committee. The soldier took them gingerly, turned them upside down and looked at them without comprehension. Evidently he could not read. He handed them back and spat on the floor. "*Bumagli!* Papers!" said he with contempt. The mass slowly began to close in, like wild cattle around a cow-puncher on foot. Over their heads I caught sight of an officer, looking helpless, and shouted to him. He made for us, shouldering his way through.

"I'm the Commissar," he said to me. "Who are you? What is it?" The others held back, waiting. I produced the papers.

"You are foreigners?" he rapidly asked in French. "It is very dangerous. . . ." Then he turned to the mob, holding up our documents. "Comrades!" he cried, "These people are foreign comrades—from America. They have come here to be able to tell their countrymen about the bravery and the revolutionary discipline of the proletarian army!"

"How do you know that?" replied the big soldier. "I tell you they are provocators! They say they came here to observe the revolutionary discipline of the proletarian army, but they have been wandering freely through the Palace, and how do we know they haven't their pockets full of loot?"

"*Pravilno!*" snarled the others, pressing forward.

"Comrades! Comrades!" appealed the officer, sweat standing out on his forehead. "I am Commissar of the Military Revolutionary Committee. Do you trust me? Well, I tell you that these passes are signed with the same names that are signed to my pass!"

He led us down through the Palace and out through a door opening on to the Neva quay, before which stood the usual committee going through pockets. . . . "You have narrowly escaped," he kept muttering, wiping his face.

"What happened to the Women's Battalion?" we asked.

"Oh—the women!" He laughed. "They were all huddled up in a back room. We had a terrible time deciding what to do with them—many were in hysterics, and so on. So finally we marched them up to the Finland Station and put them on a train to Levashovo, where they have a camp. . . .

We came out into the cold, nervous night, murmurous with obscure armies on the move, electric with patrols. From across the river, where loomed under the darker mass of Peter-Paul came a hoarse shout. . . . Underfoot the sidewalk was littered with broken stucco, from the cornice of the Palace where two shells from the battleship *Avrora* had struck; that was the only damage done by the bombardment.

It was now after three in the morning. On the Nevsky all the street-lights were again shining, the cannon gone, and the only signs of war were Red Guards and soldiers squatting around fires. The city was quiet—probably never so quiet in its history; on that night not a single hold-up occurred, not a single robbery.

But the City Duma Building was all illuminated. We mounted to the galleried Alexander Hall, hung with its great gold-framed, red-shrouded Imperial portraits. About a hundred people were grouped around the platform, where Skobeliev was speaking. He urged that the Committee of Public Safety be expanded, so as to unite all the anti-Bolshevik elements in one huge organization, to be called the Committee for Salvation of Country and Revolution. And as we looked on, the Committee for Salvation was formed—that Committee which was to develop into the most powerful enemy of the Bolsheviki, appearing, in the next week, sometimes under its own partisan name, and sometimes as the strictly non-partisan Committee of Public Safety. . . .

Dan, Gotz, Avksentiev were there, some of the insurgent Soviet delegates, members of the Executive Committee of the Peasants' Soviets, old Prokopovich, and even members of the Council of the Republic—among whom Vinaver and other Cadets. Lieber cried that the convention of the Soviets was not a legal convention, that the old Tsay-ee-kah was still in office. . . . An appeal to the country was drafted.

We hailed a cab. "Where to?" But when we said "Smolny," the *izvozchick* shook his head. *"Niet!"* said he, "there are devils. . . ." It was only after weary wandering that we found a driver willing to take us—and he wanted thirty roubles, and stopped two blocks away.

The windows of Smolny were still ablaze, motors came and went, and around the still-leaping fires the sentries huddled close, eagerly asking everybody the latest news. The corridors were full of hurrying men, hollow-eyed and dirty. In some of the committee-rooms people lay sleeping on the floor, their guns beside them. In spite of the seceding delegates, the hall of meetings was crowded with people roaring like the sea. As we came in, Kameniev was reading the list of arrested Ministers. The name of Tereshchenko was greeted with thunderous applause, shouts of satisfaction, laughter; Rutenberg came in for less; and at the mention of Palchinsky, a storm of hoots, angry cries, cheers burst forth. . . . It was announced that Chudnovsky had been appointed Commissar of the Winter Palace.

Now occurred a dramatic interruption. A big peasant, his bearded face convulsed with rage, mounted the platform and pounded with his fist on the presidium table.

"We, Socialist Revolutionaries, insist on the immediate release of the Socialist Ministers arrested in the Winter Palace! Comrades! Do you know that four comrades who risked their lives and their freedom fighting against tyranny of the Tsar, have been flung into Peter-Paul prison—the historical tomb of Liberty?" In the uproar he pounded and yelled. Another delegate climbed up beside him and pointed at the presidium.

"Are the representatives of the revolutionary masses going to sit here quietly while the Okhrana of the Bolsheviki tortures their leaders?"

Trotsky was gesturing for silence. "These 'comrades' who are now caught plotting the crushing of the Soviets with the adventurer Kerensky—is there any reason to handle them with gloves? After 16 and 18 July they didn't use much ceremony with us!" With a triumphant ring in his voice he cried, "Now that the *oborontsi* and the faint-hearted have gone, and the whole task of defending and saving the Revolution rests on our shoulders, it is particularly necessary to work—work—work! We have decided to die rather than give up!"

Followed him a Commissar from Tsarskoye Selo, panting and covered with the mud of his ride. "The garrison of Tsarskoye Selo is on guard at the gates of Petrograd, ready to defend the Soviets and the Military Revolutionary Committee!" Wild cheers. "The Cycle Corps sent from the front has arrived at Tsarskoye, and the soldiers are now with us; they recognize the power of the Soviets, the necessity of immediate transfer of land to the peasants and industrial control to the workers. The Fifth Battalion of Cyclists, stationed at Tsarskoye, is ours. . . ."

Then the delegate of the Third Cycle Battalion. In the midst of delirious enthusiasm he told how the cycle corps had been ordered *three days before* from the Southwest front to the "defence of Petrograd." They suspected, however, the meaning of the order; and at the station of

Peredolsk were met by representatives of the Fifth Battalion from Tsarskoye. A joint meeting was held, and it was discovered that "among the cyclists not a single man was found willing to shed the blood of his fathers, or to support a Government of bourgeois and landowners!"

Kapelinsky, for the Mensheviki Internationalists, proposed to elect a special committee to find a peaceful solution to the civil war. "There isn't any peaceful solution!" bellowed the crowd. "Victory is the only solution!" The vote was overwhelmingly against, and the Mensheviki Internationalists left the Congress in a whirlwind of jocular insults. There was no longer any panic fear. . . . Kameniev from the platform shouted after them, "The Mensheviki Internationalists claimed 'emergency' for the question of 'peaceful resolution,' but they always voted for suspension of the order of the day in favor of declarations of factions which wanted to leave the Congress. It is evident," finished Kameniev, "that the withdrawal of all these renegades was decided upon beforehand!"

The assembly decided to ignore the withdrawal of the factions, and proceed to the appeal to the workers, soldiers, and peasants of all Russia.

TO WORKERS, SOLDIERS, AND PEASANTS THE SECOND ALL-RUSSIAN Congress of Soviets of Workers' and Soldiers' Deputies has opened. It represents the great majority of the Soviets. There are also a number of Peasant deputies. Based upon the will of the great majority of the workers, soldiers, and peasants, based upon the triumphant uprising of the Petrograd workmen and soldiers, the Congress assumes power.

The Provisional Government is deposed. Most of the members of the Provisional Government are already arrested.

The Soviet authority will at once propose an immediate democratic peace to all nations, and an immediate truce on all fronts. It will assure the free transfer of landlord, crown, and monastery lands to the Land Committees, defend the soldiers rights, enforcing a complete democratization of the Army, establish workers' control over production, ensure the convocation of the Constituent Assembly at the proper date, take means to supply bread to the cities and articles of first necessity to the villages, and secure to all nationalities living in Russia a real right to independent existence.

The Congress resolves: that all local power shall be transferred to the Soviet of Workers', Soldiers', and Peasants' Deputies, which must enforce revolutionary order.

The Congress calls upon the soldiers in the trenches to be watchful and steadfast. The Congress of Soviets is sure that the revolutionary Army will know how to defend the Revolution against all attacks of Imperialism, until the new Government shall have brought about the conclusion of the democratic peace which it will directly propose to all nations. The new Government will take all necessary steps to secure everything needful to the revolutionary Army, by means of a determined policy of requisition and taxation of the propertied classes, and also to improve the situation of the soldiers' families.

The Kornilovtsi—Kerensky, Kaledin, and others, are endeavoring to lead troops against Petrograd. Several regiments, deceived by Kerensky, have sided with the insurgent People.

Soldiers! Make active resistance to the Kornilovets—Kerensky! Be on guard!

Railway men! Stop all troop-trains being sent by Kerensky against Petrograd!

Soldiers, Workers, Clerical employees! The destiny of the Revolution and democratic peace is in your hands!

Long live the Revolution!

The All-Russian Congress of Soviets of Workers' and Soldiers' Deputies Delegates from the Peasants' Soviets

It was exactly 5:17 a.m. when Krylenko, staggering with fatigue, climbed to the tribune with a telegram in his hand.

"Comrades! From the Northern Front. The Twelfth Army sends greetings to the Congress of Soviets, announcing the formation of a Military Revolutionary Committee which has taken over the command of the Northern Front!" Pandemonium, men weeping, embracing each other. "General Chermissov has recognized the Committee—Commissar of the Provisional Government Voitinsky has resigned!"

So. Lenin and the Petrograd workers had decided on insurrection, the Petrograd Soviet had overthrown the Provisional Government, and thrust the *coup d'état* upon the Congress of Soviets. Now there was all great Russia to win—and then the world! Would Russia follow and rise? And the world—what of it? Would the peoples answer and rise, a red world-tide?

Although it was six in the morning, night was yet heavy and chill. There was only a faint unearthly pallor stealing over the silent streets, dimming the watch-fires, the shadow of a terrible dawn grey-rising over Russia. . . .

Marquis de Custine

PETERSBURG

Petersburg, July 10, 1839

ON APPROACHING KRONSTADT, a submersed fortress of which the Russians are justly proud, one sees the Gulf of Finland suddenly come to life. The imposing ships of the Imperial Navy cover it in every direction—the Emperor's fleet. It is icebound in port during more than six months of the year, and during the three months

Globetrotting novelist Marquis de Custine first visited Russia in 1839. In this excerpt from his Journey for Our Time, *Custine warily enters the port of St. Petersburg.*

of summer the Navy cadets do their maneuvers between St. Petersburg and the Baltic Sea. Thus, they make use of the time during which the sun permits navigation in these latitudes for the instruction of youth.

The Baltic Sea with its somber shades and its little traveled waters proclaims the proximity of a continent deprived of inhabitants by the rigors of the climate. There the barren shores harmonize with the cold and empty sea. The dreariness of the earth, of the sky, and the cold tinge of the waters, chill the heart of a traveler. Almost before he touches this uninviting shore he would like to leave it. With a sigh he remembers the words of one of the favorites of the Empress Catherine when she was complaining of the effects of the Petersburg climate on her health: "It is not God's fault, Madam, if men are so obstinate as to build the capital of a great empire in a land destined by Nature to be the habitation of bears and wolves!"

My traveling companion proudly explained the recent progress of the Russian Navy. I expressed admiration for this marvel without appreciating it as they do. It is a creation, or more correctly a recreation, of the Emperor Nicholas, who enjoys realizing the dominant desire of Peter I. But however powerful a man may be, he is forced, sooner or later, to admit that Nature is stronger than man. As long as Russia does not exceed her natural limits, the Russian Navy will be the plaything of emperors—nothing more!

In spite of the courtly pride with which the Russians vaunted the miracles of the will of the master who wishes to have, and who does have, an imperial navy, from the moment I knew that the ships I saw were there solely for the instructions of students, a secret disinterest smothered my curiosity.

This activity, which does not have its compulsion in events, which is neither the result of war nor of commerce, seemed to me just a parade. But heaven and the Russians know what a pleasure a parade is! The taste for reviews is pushed in Russia to the point of madness: and behold, even before entering this empire of military maneuvers I must attend a review on the water! . . . I am not moved to laughter; puerility on a grand scale is to me an appalling thing; it is a monstrosity which is possible only under tyranny, of which it is perhaps the most terrible revelation!

Everywhere, except under absolute despotism, when men put forth great effort it is to achieve a great goal; it is only with blindly submissive peoples that a ruler can demand immense sacrifices to produce trifles.

Far from inducing the admiration expected from me here, this despotic improvisation evokes a sort of fear—not fear of war, but fear of tyranny. This useless navy of Nicholas I brings back to me all the cruelty in the heart of Peter the Great, the model of all Russian sovereigns, ancient and modern, and I ask myself where I am going? What is Russia? Russia is the country where one can do the greatest things for the most insignificant result. Don't go there!

Nothing is as sad as nature on the approach to Petersburg. As one sinks into the Gulf, the marshy Ingermanland, which steadily becomes lower, dwindles in the end to a quivering little line drawn between the sky and the sea; that line is Russia. . . . In other words, a low, humid land strewn as far as the eye can see with poor, miserable birch trees. This landscape—flat, empty, regular, without color, without bounds but even so without grandeur—is barely lighted enough to be visible. Here the gray earth is indeed worthy of the pale sun which lights it, not from above but from the sides, almost from below, as its oblique rays form such a sharp angle with the surface of the earth—stepchild of the Creator. In Russia the nights have a clarity which is astonishing, but the days have an obscurity which is depressing. The best of the days have a bluish tint.

Kronstadt with its forests of masts, its substructures, and its granite walls nobly interrupts the monotonous revery of the pilgrim who comes like me asking for pictures from this ungrateful land. I have never seen anything in the neighborhood of any big city as sad as the shores of the Neva.

Before arriving at Petersburg you cross a desert of water framed by a desert of peat bog: seas, shores, sky, everything mingles; it is like a mirror, but so muddy, so dull you would say that the glass has not been foiled, for it reflects nothing.

Such is the approach to Petersburg. In choosing this site, did all the drawbacks from the point of view of nature and the obvious needs of a great people pass through the mind of Peter the Great without impressing him? The sea at any price—that is what he said! . . . What a weird idea for a Russian to found the capital of the Empire of the Slavs on Finnish territory opposite the Swedes! It was useless for Peter the Great to say that he wished only to give Russia a port. If he was the genius he is reputed to be, he should have foreseen the full consequence of his choice; and, as for me, I do not doubt that he did foresee it. Policy and, I very much fear, the vengeance of the Czar's *amour-propre*, irritated by the independence of the old Muscovites, decided the destiny of modern Russia. The Russians in vain applaud with words the fate that has befallen them; secretly they think, just as I do, that the contrary would have been better.

Russia is like a man, full of vigor, suffocating. She lacks outlets. Peter the Great promised them to her; he opened to her the Gulf of Finland without perceiving that a sea necessarily closed eight months out of the year is not the same thing as other seas. But labels are everything for the Russians. The efforts of Peter I, of his subjects, and of his successors, astonishing as they are, have produced only a city which is difficult to inhabit, where the Neva disputes her ground with every puff of wind that leaves the Gulf and where men think of flight at every step war permits them to take toward the south. For a bivouac, wharves of granite were superfluous.

Kronstadt is a very flat island in the middle of the Gulf of Finland. This aquatic fortress rises above the sea only just enough to prevent the navigation of enemy vessels attempting an attack on Petersburg. Its dungeons, its foundations, its strength are largely under water. The artillery with which it is armed is placed, the Russians say, with great art—in a single volley each shell would tell, and the entire sea would be plowed up like earth crumbled by the plow and the harrow. Thanks to this hail of bullets that an order from the Czar can make rain at will upon the enemy, the place is considered impregnable. I do not know if these cannons can close the two passes of the Gulf; the Russians who would be able to enlighten me would not wish to do so. To answer this question, it would be necessary to calculate the carriage and the direction of the missiles and sound the depth of these two straits. My experience, however recent of date, has already taught me to distrust the empty blusterings and the exaggerations of Russians inspired by an excess of zeal for the service of their master. This national conceit would seem tolerable to me only in a free people. So much vainglory is only from fear, I tell myself; such haughtiness only a meanness ingeniously disguised. This discovery makes me hostile.

In France, as in Russia, I have met two kinds of parlor Russians: those whose discretion conspires with their vanity to praise their country beyond measure, and those who, wishing to give themselves a more elegant, a more civilized air, affect either a profound disdain or an excessive modesty every time they speak of Russia. Up to the present I have not been duped by either the one or the other; but I should like to find a third type—the completely natural Russian. I am looking for it.

We arrived at Kronstadt toward dawn on one of those fine days without beginning and without end that I am tired of describing but not tired of admiring—that is to say, about midnight. The season of these long days is short and already nearing its end.

We dropped anchor in front of the silent fortress, but we had to wait a long time for the arousing of an army of employees who came on board one after another—police commissars, directors, assistant directors of the Customs, and finally the Governor of the Customs himself. This important personage felt himself obliged to pay us a visit in honor of the illustrious Russian passengers aboard the *Nicholas I.* He talked at length with the princes and princesses who are returning to Petersburg. They spoke Russian, probably because the subject of conversation was Western European politics; but when the conversation was turned to the difficulties of landing and to the necessity of abandoning one's carriage and changing ships, they spoke French.

The Russian princes were obliged, like me, a simple foreigner, to submit to the customs laws. This equality pleased me at first, but upon arriving at Petersburg, I saw them cleared in three minutes while I had to struggle for three hours against annoyances of all kinds. Privilege, for a moment poorly disguised under the leveling process of despotism, reappeared, and I did not like this resurrection.

The profusion of small, superfluous precautions creates here a population of clerks. Each one of these men discharges his duty with a pedantry, a rigor, an air of importance uniquely designed to give prominence to the most obscure employment. He does not permit himself to say so, but you can see him thinking approximately this: "Make way for me, I am one of the members of the great machine of the State."

This member of the machine, functioning according to a will which is not his own, lives as much as the movement of a clock; however, in Russia this is called a man! The sight of these voluntary automatons frightens me. There is something supernatural in an individual reduced to the state of pure machine. If, in countries where machines abound, wood and metal seem to have a soul, under despotism men seem to be of wood. One asks oneself what they can do with their excess of thought and you feel uncomfortable at the idea of the force that had to be exerted against intelligent beings to succeed in making them only things. In Russia I pity persons as in England I feared machines. In England the creations of man lack only speech; in Russia speech is too much for the creatures of the State.

These machines inconvenienced with a soul are, however, appallingly polite; you can see that from the cradle they have been forced to civility just as much as to the handling of arms. But what value can the forms of politeness have when respect is by command? Whatever despotism may do, the free will of man will always be a necessary consecration to every human act if that act is to have significance; the ability to choose his own master can alone give value to fidelity. Since in Russia an inferior chooses nothing, nothing that he does or says has either· meaning or value.

At the sight of all these categories of spies who examined and questioned us, I was seized by a desire to yawn, which could easily have turned into a desire to weep, not for myself but for this people. So many precautions, considered indispensable here but completely dispensed with elsewhere, warned me that I was on the verge of entering an empire of fear; and fear like sadness is contagious. Thus I was afraid and I was sad . . . through politeness . . . to put myself in tune with everybody else.

I was asked to go to the saloon of our ship, where I had to appear before a tribunal of clerks assembled to question the passengers. All the members of this tribunal, more dreadful than imposing, were seated in front of a large table. Several of them leafed through registers with sinister attention. They appeared to be too absorbed not to have some secret duty to perform—their acknowledged function was not sufficient to motivate such gravity.

Some, pen in hand, listened to the responses of

the travelers, or, it would be more accurate to say, of the accused, for all foreigners are treated as criminals upon arrival at the Russian frontier. Others dictated in a loud voice to copyists words to which we attached no importance; these words were translated from language to language, from French to German and finally to Russian, at which point the last of the scribes entered them irrevocably and perhaps arbitrarily in his book. They copied the names inscribed on the passports; each date, each visa was examined with minute care; but the passenger, persecuted by this mental torture, was never questioned except in phrases of which the extremely polite form seemed to me calculated to console one in the dock.

The result of the long interrogation, to which I, like the others, was subjected, was that they took my passport after making me sign a card which would enable me, I was told, to reclaim my passport at St. Petersburg.

Everybody seemed to have satisfied the formalities prescribed by the police. The trunks and the passengers were already on the new boat. For four hours by the clock we had been languishing in front of Kronstadt and, as yet, nothing had been said about leaving.

Every minute new black skiffs came out of the city and rowed sadly toward us. Although we had anchored very near the walls of the city, there was a deep silence. Not a sound came out of this tomb. The shadows one saw sailing around it were as mute as the stones they had just left. One would have said like a convoy prepared for a corpse that was keeping it waiting. The men who managed these lugubrious, dirty little boats were clad in heavy gray woolen storm-coats and their faces lacked expression; their eyes were lifeless and their complexion of a jaundiced yellow. I was told that they were the sailors attached to the garrison, and they looked like soldiers. It had long been broad day, but there was scarcely more light than at dawn, and the sun, still not high but reflecting on the water, bothered me. Sometimes small boats turned around us in silence without anyone coming on board; other times six or twelve ragged seamen, half covered with inverted sheepskin—the wool inside and the filthy leather outside—brought us a new police agent, or an officer of the garrison, or a tardy customs officer. These goings and comings, which did not further our business, at least gave me leisure for sad reflections on the kind of filth particular to men of the North. People of the South spend their lives in the open air, half-naked, or in the water; whereas, people of the North are nearly always shut up and have a deep, oily dirtiness that seems to me much more repulsive than the negligence of the peoples destined to live under the sky and born to warm themselves under the sun.

The tiresomeness to which the Russian minutiae condemned us also gave us occasion to note that the grandees of the land are not very long-suffering with regard to the inconveniences of the public order when this order weighs on them.

"Russia is the land of useless formalities," they murmured among themselves, but in French lest they be understood by subordinate employees. I have remembered this observation as my own experience has already proven the justice of it only too well. From what I have been able to find out up to now, a book entitled *Russians Judged by Themselves* would be severe—love of their country is for them only a means of flattering the ruler. As soon as they think the ruler cannot hear them, they speak of everything with a frankness which is all the more dreadful because those who listen share the responsibility. The reason for so much delay was finally revealed to us. The chief of chiefs, the superior of superiors, the director of directors of the customs officers appeared. Instead of confining himself to wearing a uniform, this supreme functionary appeared in a dress coat like a private individual. It seems that his rôle is to play the man of the world. Our drawing-room customs officer, all the while giving himself airs of the court, politely confiscated a parasol, took away a dressing-case, took custody of a trunk, and renewed, with an imperturbable *sang-froid,* the searches already conscientiously made by his subordinates.

In the Russian administration the minutiae do not eliminate disorder. They take a great deal of trouble to achieve a small end, and they believe they can never do enough to prove their ardor. The result of this emulation of clerks is that one formality does not insure the traveler against another. It is like pillage—the fact that the traveler has escaped from the hands of one band is no reason to say he will not encounter a second and a third; and all these gangs, spaced along his route, pester him to their hearts' content.

The more or less scrupulous conscience of these employees of all grades with whom the traveler can have to do decides his fate. It is useless to speak if one has a complaint against an employee, for a complaint will never be in order. And this is a country, thus administered, which wishes to be considered civilized in the same sense as the states of the Occident.

The supreme chief of the jailers of the Empire proceeded slowly to examine the ship. He took a long time, a very long time, to fulfill his duty. The necessity of keeping up a conversation is a burden which complicates the functions of this musky guardian—musky in the literal sense, for one can smell the musk a mile away. At last we finished with the customs ceremonies, the courtesies of the police, were rid of the military salutes and a spectacle of the most profound misery which can mar the human race, for the oarsmen of the gentlemen of the Russian Customs are creatures of a kind apart. As I could do nothing for them, their presence was odious to me, and each time these miserable wretches brought to the ship officials of all grades employed by the Customs Service and by the Maritime Police—the most severe police of the Empire—I turned my eyes. These ragged seamen are a disgrace to their country; they are a species of greasy galley slaves who spend their lives transporting the clerks and officials of Kronstadt aboard foreign vessels. In seeing their faces and in thinking about what is called existence for these poor devils, I asked myself what man has done to God that sixty million of the human race should be condemned to live in Russia.

Francine du Plessix Gray

MAYA

IT WAS EVIDENT from the moment I walked into their living room that Maya and Yuri Krassin's marriage was not doing well.

Maya and Yuri live in the periphery of Leningrad, in one of those vast complexes of already disintegrating housing units, 1970s vintage, that express the bleakness of even the more privileged Soviet lives. The couple's

During the 1980s, journalist Francine du Plessix Gray traveled the Russian countryside, speaking to housewives, actresses, journalists—all shapes and sizes of Russian women. She collected it all in her astounding 1990 volume, Soviet Women: Walking the Tightrope.

careers—Yuri is a computer engineer, Maya a journalist with aspirations of writing fiction—afford them living quarters which by Soviet standards can be called spacious. Upon arriving at their flat, in which they have lived for four years, one enters a corridor that gives onto a kitchen, a modest room that serves as Yuri's study, and two small bedrooms. Straight ahead, there is a fairly commodious living-and-dining area some forty feet square.

I had been invited to the Krassins' at 6 P.M. for a light Sunday supper. I was struck, upon entering their living room, that this space could not be called a home, that there was no love in it, that its bleakness could come only from a woman's total dearth of caring. The room was furnished with one ancient couch in front of which stood a low, dilapidated coffee table. There was not a chair or armchair in it, no pictures on the wall, no furnishings of any kind, in fact, save for an expensive stereo set of German make placed directly upon the dusty, uncarpeted floor. It occurred to me that this was a new breed of Russian woman I was meeting in Maya, that throughout my several stays in the Soviet Union I had not yet been in one home which so radically lacked the traditional Slavic sense of *uyutnost'*.

For there was none of that traditional gift in Yuri and Maya's bleak flat. All decoration was reserved for Maya, a trim woman with carefully coiffed dark hair and a pert, expertly made-up face, who wore, that evening, a turquoise silk dress and quite a bit of gold costume jewelry. As she moved about her bare uncarpeted rooms, her very high heels made a nervy clickety-clack sound which seemed to disturb Yuri—but then, Yuri seemed disturbed by most anything his wide did or said that evening. He is a solidly built man in his early thirties with scholarly spectacles, a reddish beard, and long, thinning hair. Upon greeting us, he had brought in some chairs from the kitchen for us to sit on. And then he had gruffly plunked himself down on one of them, his torso bent tersely forward, his sleeves rolled up above powerful forearms, which were strewn with faint lacerations, as if he'd fallen into a patch of thorny bushes. His blue eyes expressed little else than anger, impatience, and a piteous vulnerability.

Maya, who immediately struck me as a very voluble person, began the conversation with a statement that citizens of earlier Soviet regimes would have found shocking: She was fed up with being a working woman. She wished just to sit home and write. Maya enjoyed working only when the work was *fulfilling,* when it was a *beloved,* freely chosen work. And she immediately launched into a paean to American life: How wonderful, she said to me, that your women can work only *when they choose,* that they are not *forced* to work as women are in the Soviet Union—that was her impression of our system. Constantly interrupting my attempts to explain that millions of women in the United States have to work out of necessity, she went on to lavish praise on that particular aspect of the American way.

I asked Maya what kind of attitude—envy or disdain—was felt by members of her generation toward Soviet women who were not employed full time. Maya's pace thereupon slowed a bit. She couldn't think of *any* woman who was not employed full time . . . except of course the ones who stayed home to take care of their babies, that was the custom of the country, partly paid leave until the child is one year old . . . but no, she had no friends who'd ever stayed home except to take care of a small child . . . as for attitude . . . how did she feel about unemployed women? Envy, of course! And so did all her friends! Who could not envy a woman who didn't have to break her back "for the sole sake of keeping a family fed?"

Throughout this tirade against one of the most central values of the 1917 Revolution—full employment, the universal right to work regardless of gender—Yuri had stayed hunched in his chair, his nails digging nervously into his squat, powerful hands.

"I saw an American movie recently about a couple in which the wife earns the family income and the husband stays home to take care of the family," he said in his low, rugged voice. "It looked like an interesting option."

Maya waved disdainfully toward her spouse, as if he had uttered a total idiocy. "How can there be anything good about such a reversal of roles—the woman becoming a man and the man becoming a woman? Nature made us different, and for good reasons." She turned toward her husband and curtly said, "Do go and put the tea kettle on, won't you?"

Yuri shuffled out of the room, his body angry and coiled, as Maya continued: "Not long ago a friend of mine, a very brilliant man, asked me a question which I thought over for a long, long time. 'What is most lacking to Soviet women?' he asked. I thought about this a lot, because writing novels, of course, is a way for us to answer such questions . . . "

Yuri returned to his chair in time to hear Maya speak the following words: ". . . so after thinking a lot, I decided that what Soviet women lack most of all is a pleasant little dependence, a voluntary dependence, on some beloved man who is stronger and wiser than they are . . ."

Yuri hunched forward even more angrily on his chair, his eyes on the floor. I stared at the scars on his arms. There was blood in the air, the heat of a day-long argument still glowed in the room.

". . . Yes," Maya continued, "Soviet women miss not being able to depend on a beloved man. You know, in this country it was always thought that man speaks with God directly, and woman only speaks with God through her man. And if the men could come a little closer to God, there would be more happy Soviet women. But above all, in Soviet society, there are many women who don't have a good strong man next to them, a man through whom they could come closer to God. For that she would need a man who is a leader, and she can't find him . . ."

Yuri sprung up, his body straightening up like a jack-in-the-box. "And what would happen then?" he cried out angrily. "What would happen . . ."

"Don't interrupt me," Maya snapped. "The smarter the woman, the harder to find a man who's higher, wiser, stronger than she is, and we can't find such . . ."

This time I was impelled to interrupt her. "Why can't we love men who're our equals?" I asked. "What in heck would be wrong with that?"

"Because the man must always remain the intellectual leader," she answered me with a coquettish smile. "He must remain smarter. If his wife is on the same level as he, then she will feel sorry for him, and pity is a motherly emotion, merely that we feel for a wounded child. . . ."

"So that's the way you're putting it!" Yuri returned to the fray. "As those reactionary princes said in Turgenev's novels, the more education a woman has, the less chances she has of being happy?"

But Maya didn't want to let go of her education, about which she had already boasted much to me. She simply wanted her spouse to earn more money than she did (a curiously conservative desire, I thought, in most of today's cultures).

"It appears to me," she answered him, quite cordially this time, "that when men and women started being equal in our society, that's when the disharmony, the unbalance began. All I'm saying is that a man should always remain a *tiny, tiny* bit ahead of his woman."

It was such an adorable Russian term she'd used for "tiny," *"chut' chut',"* the word used for phrases such as "I only want the weeniest drop of cream in my coffee."

"That's a very delicate culinary balance you're asking for," I butted in, "a very complex recipe. That's like asking life to be a perfect soufflé."

"But your husband is an artist," Maya suggested daintily. "Perhaps when both spouses are engaged in creative work you can't compare their levels, you can't say who's better or stronger . . ."

"And science?" Yuri demanded, his furious bushy head turned straight toward his wife's this time. "Isn't science creative work?"

"Well, inventors are creative," Maya said diffidently. "That's something else."

"And where do you draw the line between invention and creative interpretation?" he demanded again.

"Yuri," she said crisply, "can you bring the things for tea? The kettle's boiling."

Yuri trundled out of the room again. He came back with a tray laden with egg salad, radishes, and sliced cucumbers, a cake, and set it on the coffee table in front of us. It was the first time I'd seen a Soviet man bring food in from the kitchen. As Maya fussed over the remarkably dry, flavorless cake, announcing with pride that it was "the first time all year" she'd baked one, she asked me the age of my children, bade her husband bring a photograph of their ten-year-old son, who was at Pioneer Camp that day, and asked to see photographs of my own family.

A brief calm hung over the frugal, satisfying snack as Maya talked about her career. She detested her job at the newspaper, where she was assigned to the "Youth Page" and made to write reports on such dreary subjects as Komsomol activities. She had an awful schedule, 9 A.M. to 6 P.M., and then the hours of commuting and standing in line for groceries, she was seldom home before 8 P.M. . . . the only interesting part of her life was the fiction she wrote at home in her spare time. She had sold one story entitled "French Silk Stockings" to a Leningrad literary journal. She was hard at work on two others, called "The Countess" and "The Passionate Flame." Ah, if she could only sit home and "express herself" through writing all day long, she would be happy to work sixteen, eighteen hours a day . . .

I suddenly realized I'd already known many prototypes of Maya: The frustrated women I'd met at writing workshops at Berkeley, Indiana, Duke University, since the 1960s, when our own cult of self-expression boomed. . . . I sprung out of my reverie on American cults of self to hear my hosts engaged in still another angry argument.

"Why always load the blame on men for your unhappiness?" Yuri was saying. "The way it's turning out, the more I earn the more I'm going to be esteemed, the more I help out at home the less you respect me. That's precisely what you're saying, aren't you?"

Yuri's gambit didn't work. Maya had a great talent for changing the issue whenever her true intentions were in danger of being disclosed.

"But *perestroika* is offering us so many new possibilities!" she said, turning to me with another ravishing smile. "Our friend Misha, for instance, has started a cooperative for designing wallpaper and upholstery fabric; he's made such a pile he's expanding into all areas of interior decorating. And Vadim, our neighbor down the block, has started a poodle-breeding cooperative, he's making money hand over fist. So there are all these new possibilities, these guys are using their initiative, supporting their families better . . ."

(I was beginning to read Maya's subtext: "Yuri, you lazy lout, why don't *you* get your fat ass off your computer chair and make some extra money?")

". . . Earlier a man wasn't allowed to use his initiative in such ways," Maya continued; "he'd have to compromise himself working *na levo*, illegally. Now he can make a lot of money in total honesty . . ."

"It's a contradiction of socialism," Yuri muttered.

"Nothing bad in *that*," Maya said firmly.

"Cooperatives are the only way of improving our society."

Well, that was as good a moment as any to ask Maya the question I'd been posing throughout a half-dozen Soviet cities. What would be the main impact of *perestroika* on the lives of women? Maya was ready to go to town on that.

"It'll offer husbands the possibility to earn more money, to free women to work as much as they *want,* not as much as they *must.* Oh, how we need that! Most of my women friends leave the house at seven-thirty, as I do, and don't get home until eight. They don't have the time to see their mothers, their children . . ."

"You see," Maya added, lighting a cigarette with a serious air, "up to now self-sacrifice has been the central motive of Russian women, that is, after all, the central theme of our literature; but at last we're fed up with being martyrs and heroines, we want fairness, justice . . ."

"And what about the husband," Yuri butted in, "what about us? Men also come home from work after having struggled all day . . ."

"The way Turgenev saw it . . ." Maya tried to interrupt.

"What you're saying," Yuri cut her off, "is that a woman is solely made happy by her husband's money. Well, I recently saw a film in which there's a woman whose husband has such a good job that she can stay home with nothing to do. And guess what happens? She runs off with a *sportsman* and begins to steal French perfume from shops. Out of egoism and boredom, sheer boredom. Without work a woman simply doesn't know what to do with herself . . ."

Now I was reading Yuri's subtext: Leisure, craving for decadent Western goods—demise of the socialist dream—woman's demonic energies becoming uncontrollable when not channeled into the work collective—a threat to the well-being of the state . . . It was Maya's turn to grow livid. She lightly slapped her husband's arm with a paper napkin.

"Foul play!" she raged. "Just because I've written a story called 'French Silk Stockings!' All I'm saying is that a woman has to have a choice. She can only retain her spiritual center when she makes a decision from within, whereas when she's *forced* into work she becomes capable of doing anything . . ."

"It all leads to egoism," Yuri repeated. "I want this, I want that, this one has this trip and that dress I don't have, I want it too . . ."

I looked down a the coffee table and stared at the photograph of the Krassins' son, so earnest and smiling in his blue-and-red Pioneer uniform. Another victim of the divorce-plagued Soviet family? Maya had forgetfully set glasses and cups all over the photo. Yuri stood up, removed it from the table, wiped it clean, carefully placed it back into the bookcase.

Noticing her negligence, Maya went to the bookshelf and handed me two of her short stories, "The Countess," "French Silk Stockings."

"Interesting titles," I said. "But listen, why can't you share things more evenly? Vacations, for instance. If a woman earns as much as a man, why not take turns? One year he chooses the vacation, another year she chooses, she can even go on her vacation *without* her man."

"You should go into marriage counseling," Yuri said, with a touch of gratitude.

"Remember how it was in the good old days," Maya continued dreamily. "The men worked and brought home the money, the women took care of the house. Two basic functions. Women don't *want* to do men's work . . ."

"Don't you have women supporting families in the United States?" Yuri turned to me with his blue, wounded eyes.

"Yes," I said, "mostly in black families. Russian society is very similar to that of our blacks . . ."

"We are like *blacks!*" husband and wife said loudly in unison.

". . . Very strong women holding many families together," I continued. "Whereas in our white households, husbands and fathers often have far stronger roles."

Yuri seemed impelled to return to economics. "Well, it turns out that the most important thing for our women is money, material goods. We're not satisfied any more living in communal apartments, we all want cars. . . ."

The evening would have ended like most social gatherings I'd attended in the Soviet Union. At some moment, the wife inevitably says, as Maya did that night: "Women here have a double life, a double shift, they're equally exhausted by work and home, it's very sad, there has to be a way of freeing our time . . ." But Yuri offered an unusual finale.

He went to his study and returned with a manuscript in hand, announcing: "My wife keeps saying that she's a writer, but I'm a writer, too."

"Yuri, you'd better not read anything," Maya giggled nervously.

But Yuri sat down and read his story, which consisted of a telephone conversation between two men. "Victor," it began, "how are things today?" "Not bad, old pal, I stood in line an hour for two quarts of milk, and another hour for a piece of chicken." "Well, the old girl should be very pleased with you, what are you cooking for dinner tonight?" "I thought I'd try a cutlet Kiev with a cucumber garnish on the side . . ."

"Two writers in one house are just too much," Maya interrupted after the first paragraph. "Yuri! Please don't try to be a writer . . ."

Yuri curtly said good-bye, put on a parka, and went (or pretended he was going) to a meeting of his work collective.

I asked Maya which bus I should take to get back to my hotel at the other end of town.

Maya helped me with my coat. As I was leaving her apartment she showed me a little white hamster scrambling about a cage in her kitchen. It stared at us with angry yellow eyes and raged against the glass walls of the cage, thumping its paws at the translucent windows of its prison.

"I look at him and think: 'Soviet women!'" Maya said.

She wanted to walk me to the bus stop. As we

went down the dusty, fish-smelling stairs crowded with half-broken sleds and discarded tires, to the grim playground dotted with rickety swings and slides, Maya continued talking about the hamster: Her son had wanted the hamster so badly, it was in a certain month when they didn't have the money for such a luxury; his grandmother bought it for him. Maya was so moved by her mother's generosity that she'd sat down on the kitchen stool and cried, staring at the beautiful little white animal.

"And my son is a man of the future!" she exclaimed. "He has initiative! The hamsters had babies, his classmates all admired them and wanted one, so he sold the babies to his classmates for thirty kopecks apiece and made three rubles in a week! At the age of ten! A true *perestroika* capitalist, right?"

D. A. Orekhov

PETER THE GREAT AND THE STONEMASON

ONCE UPON A beautiful time, Peter the Great surveyed Petersburg. He drove by Putilov's mountain and saw a stonemason. Drives up to him, asks, "God be with you, fellow. How's work? Are you earning much?"

"Such trifles deserve no thanks; in a day eighty kopecks I'll earn."

The fable "Peter the Great and the Stonemason" can be traced to the times of Peter himself (1672–1725). D. A. Orekhov, a contemporary of the Czar and a fisherman by profession, is the most famous teller of the story. This is his version, translated by Nicholas Burlakoff.

"So, does this suffice?"

"It really does not suffice."

"It's a strange matter; how do you dispose of the money?"

"Twenty percent I pay to the house, 20 percent I lend out, 20 percent I throw out of the window."

The sovereign became thoughtful.

"Explain, fellow," says he, "I do not understand."

"You see, on 20 percent I feed my father and mother; on 20 percent two sons I raise; 20 percent I give to two swans [daughters]—their wings shall become firm, that's all I'll see of them. And 20 percent I keep.

"And have you ever seen the sovereign?"

"Well, no, but I would like to."

"Well, come with me. I'll show him to you. When he arrives at the village all the people will be without caps; the only one with a cap will be the sovereign."

They arrive at the village. There everybody yelled hurrah and threw their caps in the air. Peter asks, "Which one of us is the Czar? All are without hats, only we two have our hats."

"I don't know," the mason says. Then the fellow falls on his knees. "Forgive me," he says, "your Czarist majesty."

"I'll take you to Petersburg, and you'll tell your riddle to the senators."

They sat down in a cart and set off to Petersburg. On their arrival Peter the Great summoned the senators and said to them, "Well, mister senators, this peasant gave me a riddle I could not solve. I ask you to solve it in three days' time."

So the peasant told them the riddle. "I earn eighty kopecks: twenty kopecks I pay to the house, twenty I lend out, twenty kopecks I throw out the window, and on twenty kopecks I live."

"Mister senators, figure out where his money is

going. And you, fellow, don't you dare tell them without my presence."

The senators thought, guessed, but could not find a solution. Time is running out, but they can't solve the riddle. So one decided to trick him [the peasant].

"Let's call him and offer him anything he asks."

They called him and started to bribe him, but he wasn't slow. He had a large hat with a wide brim. "Fill my hat up, full of gold."

So they filled it up. Then he said, "Twenty kopecks—father and mother I feed; twenty kopecks—two sons I raise; twenty kopecks—two swans I raise; on twenty kopecks I myself live."

The senators see that the answer is the simplest, but they couldn't guess it alone. When the time was up they went to the sovereign.

"So this is the solution," they say.

He says, "You could not have solved it by yourself. He [the peasant] told you."

So they confessed. How sternly he looked at the peasant. While that one says, "Your imperial majesty, just see how many of your likenesses they gave me. How could I refuse to talk?" (*You see on every gold piece there is a likeness of the sovereign.*)

They all went to dinner. The Czar sat the peasant down by his side. The senators decided to undermine him. One hit his neighbor and said "Pass it on." So each hit in turn until it came to the peasant. He now must hit the Czar.

But he [the peasant] stood up and said, "Well, mister senators, I had this dream. The old lady and I went to the forest and saw good firewood. So we went on and started to sink. The further we go the more we sink. So maybe we should return home? Yes, I say— turn back, but the firewood is so good! Well, mister senators, what should I do, sink or turn home?"

Well, they answer, "Of course, turn back home."

He turns around and hits one [the senator who had hit him]. "Pass it on," he says.

Immediately the Czar made him the chief senator and put the others under him.

Marie Bashkirtseff

PETERSBURG

FRIDAY, 4 AUGUST (23 July, Russian style)

I went to see the train arrive and by chance my uncle was there. But he could not stay more than a quarter of an hour because at the Russian border at Wirballen he had had trouble obtaining a passport to come here, and he had given his word of honor to a customs officer to come back with the next train.

Marie Bashkirtseff was born in the Ukraine in 1858. As a young girl she moved to Nice and started what would become a behemoth 102-volume personal diary. Up to this point, these papers have only been seen in a heavily edited form, but will be published complete next fall.

Chocolat ran to find my aunt; there were only a few minutes. When she arrived, we had time only to say two words. My aunt in her worry for me, as we reentered the hotel, imagined that she had remarked in Étienne a strange air, and by such hints she discouraged me so much that I got anxious too. Finally, at midnight I got into the carriage; my aunt cried; I held my eyes high and immobile to keep the tears back. The conductor gave the signal and for the first time in my life, I found myself alone [except for Chocolat and Amalia].

"Enough, my girl," I said, getting up. It was time I was in Russia. Descending, I was received into the arms of my uncle, of two policemen, and of two customs officers. They treated me like a princess and didn't even look at my baggage. The station is large, the functionaries are elegant and excessively polite. I believed myself in an ideal country, everything, everything is good. A simple policeman here is better than an officer in France. And here let me remark in justification of our poor Emperor, who is accused of having strange eyes. Everyone who wears a helmet (and they aren't a few at Wirballen) has eyes like the Emperor. I don't know if that comes from the weight of the helmet that falls on the eyes, or from imitation. As to imitation, it's like in France where every soldier looked like Napoleon.

My compatriots don't awaken any particular emotion in me—no species of ecstasy as I have felt in seeing again a country I have already seen, but I feel great sympathy towards them and a great feeling of well being returns to me.

And then everything is so well arranged, everyone is so polite; the countenance of each Russian is all cordiality, goodness, frankness, that I have a glad heart.

Étienne came to wake me this morning at 10. The locomotives are stoked with wood so we are spared the horrible smuttiness of coal smoke. I woke up all refreshed and passed the day chatting, sleeping, and looking out the window at our beautiful Russia, so flat, but this country recalls that around Rome.

At 9:30 it was still light. We had passed Gadtchina, the ancient residence of Paul I, [who was] so persecuted during the life of his superb mother, and finally we were at Tzarskoe-Selo, and in 25 minutes at Petersburg.

I went to the Hotel Demouth, accompanied by an uncle, a maid, a black, followed by lots of baggage, and with 50 roubles in my pocket. What would you say?

While I had supper in my good sized salon—it has no carpet and no paintings on the ceiling—I thought about the prediction of the somnambulist and imagined Antonelli already throwing himself at my feet, when Étienne entered.

"Guess who is here, who is at my house?" he asked.

"No, who?"

"Guess, princess."

"I don't know."

"All right, little queen. It's Paul Issayevitch; can he come in?"

"Yes, let him in."

Paul is in Petersburg with the Governor-General of Wilna, M. Albedinsky, who married the Emperor's old mistress.

He received my telegram from Eydtkuhnen at the moment of leaving. Unable to leave, he told a friend, the Count Mouravieff, to come to meet me. But this Count has been troubled in vain, seeing that we passed Wilna at 3 at night and I was sleeping like the blessed.

Who will deny my goodness after I have said that I was gay this evening because I felt Issayevitch was happy to see me? Is that egoism? I enjoyed particularly the pleasure that I gave to another. Finally, I have a cavalier to serve me in Petersburg. I am in Petersburg. . . but I haven't yet seen anything but *droshki.* The *droshki* is a vehicle with one seat, with eight springs (like Binder's great carriages) and one horse. I saw the cathedral of Kasan with its colonnade in the style of St. Peter's in Rome, and many "drinking houses."

It's 3 in the morning and already daylight.

On all sides I hear the praises of Princess Marguerite—"So simple, so good!" they say. Simple, no one appreciates simplicity in a woman who is not a princess; be simple and good and amiable without being a queen and one's inferiors will take liberties, while your equals will say: "Good little person!" and will much prefer women who are neither simple nor good.

Oh, if I were queen! They would adore me, it is I who would be popular.

The Italian princess, her husband and her suite have not yet left Russia; they are at Kiev now. "The mother of all Russian cities," as the great prince St. Waldemar said after he became Christian and had baptized half of Russia in the Dneiper. Kiev is the richest town in the world in churches, convents, monks, and relics; and the precious stones those convents possess are fabulous; they have cellars full of them as in the stories of the Thousand and One Nights. I saw Kiev when I was 9 and I still remember the subterranean corridors, filled with relics, which run right around the town, which pass under all the streets and link all the convents with each other *underground,* creating also kilometers lined to right and left with the tombs of saints. God forgive me for a bad thought . . . I don't think that there could possibly be so many saints.

SATURDAY, 5 AUGUST (24 July)

We have been to pick up my trunks at customs. We have crossed corridors, rooms, offices; we have seen customs men of all sorts! They searched all the trunks; I undid the wrapping for them, handling the dresses and hats, hoping to moderate their zeal and prove to them that I was not a fashion merchant.

In vain I look for Russia. Everything in this hotel is German. We had lunch in the garden which is in the court of honor. Then I dressed and we went to look for the Sapogenikoffs. The coachman was hesitating again between two houses when I was lifted out of the carriage by Giro and Marie who dashed into the street when they saw us from the window. Leaving Paul and my uncle with Nina, I rushed into the girls' bedroom and for an hour it was total confusion, a babbling, shouting, like the time of Girofla.

I took them with me. We crossed the Neva in 2 boats—in the first boat, the 3 graces. In the second, the men and Chocolat. If there is anything of beauty in Petersburg, it is this superb river, large like a lake, its waters so clear and transparent one can see the bottom. I am proud to speak Russian as one more language, and these Russian animals don't appreciate my noble efforts.

Nina came to meet us and the gentlemen left us. My graces were conducted home and Nina stayed to sleep with me. It is 4. We looked at my dresses. It seems a pleasure to stay up sometimes and do something forbidden. But little by little Nina began to talk to me about things one never speaks to young girls about, and wrongly. One of her remarks struck me as just. It is that a woman in giving herself to a man, even if he is her husband, suffers a sort of humiliation because she feels the man's strength and impunity, and her own abasement since she submits. The man performs a sovereign act; the woman is only a passive instrument, whatever love there may be. The man as soon as he is satisfied sees in the woman a poor little thing to whom he has given everything, and he loves her a little for the pleasure that she has given him. But that is past, that is finished, and he gets up as if nothing has happened, while for the woman . . . it is different, and I can judge *from very far away* by what I remember of myself after the horseback ride with Antonelli, when he went very calmly to his club. Besides it is almost natural: the man gives and the woman receives. So that's love to her—the memory. Then, she has diminished the man by a certain quantity of . . . of . . . of fluid, which must act on her and by which she is augmented, morally even. But that is not *right.* It should be give and take. [Written sideways on this page later: "At the time I wrote this I didn't understand even half of what I was saying."]

Men marry, after all; they pose as wise, settled, calm, and are revolted at the least wildness in the woman. Is that right? Does it make sense?

The men settle down because they are disgusted with the contrary, but the women, all new, must they, can they be disgusted too? The man is all used up and tired and he brings to a young girl the beautiful left-overs of his mind and body. He is tired. He takes a wife to rest himself. He demands a domestic, who will not go out into the world herself, who is content with her rags, is that reasonable? I'm not advocating the depravation of women, but I demand justice and indulgence. [blotted words] innocent, I don't mix in the concerns of others where I know nothing. Competent people, just people, am I right?

Sunday, 6 August (25 July)

Instead of visiting the churches, I slept in, and Nina took me to breakfast at her house. Her parrot talked, her daughters cried, and I sang, just like in Nice. The two-seated carriage gave shelter to the three graces, who went through a pouring rain to see the cathedral of Issakie, famous for its malachite and lapis-lazuli columns. These columns have an extreme richness but are in bad taste because the green of the malachite and the blue of the lapis lazuli clash with each other.

The mosaics and the paintings are ideal, the true figures of the saints, the Virgin, and the angels. The whole church is of marble, the four facades with their granite columns are beautiful, but they are not in harmony with the gilded Byzantine dome. And in general I have a painful response to the whole exterior because the dome is too dominant and overwhelms the four little domes of the façade, which without that would be very beautiful. The profusion of gold and ornaments in the interior produces the happiest effect; the bizarre is harmonious and in the best taste, except for the two lapis-lazuli columns that would be superb elsewhere.

They were celebrating a popular marriage. The couple was ugly, and we didn't stay long to look. I love the Russian people—good, brave, loyal, naïve. These men and women stop in front of each church and each chapel, before every niche with an image, and cross themselves and stand in the middle of the street as if they were at home.

After the cathedral of Issakie we went on to that of Kasan. Another wedding, and a charming bride. This cathedral is built in imitation of St. Peter's in Rome, but the colonnade doesn't seem to be attached to the building and is not long enough to form a semi-circle; all this gives a disadvantageous and incomplete shape to the monument.

Farther on along the Nevsky, the statue of Catherine the Great; and in front of the Senate near the Winter Palace, which is merely a large barracks, the equestrian statue of Peter the Great, one hand showing the Senate, the other the Neva. The people interpret this double action rather strangely. The Tzar, they say, shows the Senate with one hand and the river with the other to say that it is better to drown in the Neva than to argue in the Senate.

The statue of Nicolas is remarkable in that it is not supported by the two [hind] legs and the tail of the horse, three supports, but only by the legs; this marvel made me reflect sadly. The communards [Nihilists] will have less to do, the support of the tail lacking.

It rains and I have a cold. I wrote to Maman: "Petersburg is filthy! The paving stones are atrocious for a capital. The Winter Palace is a barracks, and so is the Grand Theater. The cathedrals are rich but misshapen and hard to understand."

And add to all that the climate and you will have the complete effect.

MONDAY, 7 AUGUST (26 July)

Having taken Marie with me and Étienne with us, I went to look for the Princess Galitzine and Mme Voyeikoff. Both are on vacation.

After dinner we went to the Isles and the point from which we admired the sunset and the Gulf of Finland. The ravishing little Russian style villas built in wood charmed me. Situated as they are in the middle of gardens and on the shores of the mouths of the Neva, they seem like toy houses sold in a box complete with little trees made of moss and horses of wood and some lakes and ponds in glass.

We arrived after sunset and it was cold. I can't get used to this cold in July. There were few people, a few cocottes.

As Jesus felt something detach itself from him when the sick woman touched his clothes and was cured,

so I felt the fluid which flowed to Issayevitch leave me in proportion as he became more and more amorous. It is a strange feeling, that of feeling how little by little one makes oneself loved.

Étienne stayed at the house and I went with Marie, accompanied by Paul and the faithful Chocolat on the seat, with the intention of bringing Nina again to stay for the night.

Having found Giro in bed, I stayed a while with her; a word made us talk about Rome, and I told them my adventures in that city, with fire and gestures. I stopped only to laugh and Giro and Marie rolled in their beds.

An incomparable trio. I never laugh like that except with my graces.

And by a sudden if not natural reaction, I fell into melancholy on my return. Nina spoke of love, Issayevitch could ask nothing better, and I proceeded, *me*, to say that I had discovered that it was not worth the trouble to live if one did not love someone above [everything]; while not having loved yet, I was looking for an ideal.

"Have you found it?" Issayevitch asked excitedly.

"No."

All my words are received like oracles. Besides I have always done this in the past without thinking about it, and I always will in the future, but I will measure my words because I often say silly things and people take them seriously.

TUESDAY, 8 AUGUST (27 July)

We stayed up until 4. I am tired and Issayevitch was not admitted at my awakening.

Paul, my brother, telegraphed that my father sent him to look for me at Kanatof (a station on the railroad, near my uncle's place); he asks when I shall arrive.

I went straight to Nina's where I passed the whole day. The city is on holiday, and at Peterhoff the Imperial family will receive its relatives—the royal houses of Denmark and of Greece—with pomp. All of Petersburg is there to see the illumination. But not being a part *of the festivities* and not liking to be, like all of Petersburg, a specta-

tor at the rope, I stayed at Nina's and embroidered a band of tapestry imitating the Gobelins on a pale blue background. This band will be placed on the front of a dress in cream velvet, and it will be something that no one else has ever seen before for beauty and richness.

"Domum mansit, lanam fecit."

I got home at midnight with Étienne. Issayevitch came in the afternoon and I so mistreated him, aided by my graces, that he went away very sad from what my uncle said.

Petersburg acts upon me at night. I know nothing more superb than the Neva trimmed with lanterns contrasting with the moon and the deep blue, almost grey sky. The defects of houses, of pavements, of bridges are melted at night by the obliging shadows. The width of the wharfs stands out in all its majesty. The peak of the admiralty disappears in the sky and in a blue haze bordered by lights one sees the dome and the graceful shape of the cathedral of Issakie, that looks itself like a shadow or halo floating in the sky.

I would like to be here in **winter.**

Leo Tolstoy

FATHER SERGIUS

IN THE 1840S there took place in St Petersburg an event which caused general surprise: a handsome prince, commander of the sovereign's squadron of a regiment of cuirassiers, whom everyone expected to become an *aide-de-camp* and have a brilliant career at the court of Nicholas I, a month before his marriage to a beautiful lady-in-waiting who enjoyed the special favour of the empress, suddenly

Russian realism is defined by the novels of Leo Tolstoy, whose legendary tomes include War and Peace *and* Anna Karenina. Father Sergius, *from his collection* Master and Man and Other Stories, *dates from the 1880s, when Tolstoy's stories became overwhelmed by religious and philosophical tension.*

resigned his commission, broke with his fiancée, made over his modest estate to his sister, and retired to a monastery with the intention of becoming a monk. To those who knew nothing of the circumstances the whole thing was odd and unaccountable, but for Prince Stepan Kasatsky himself it was all so natural that he could not conceive of any other possible course of action.

Stepan Kasatsky's father, a retired guards colonel, had died when his son was twelve. Much as the boy's mother regretted sending him away, she felt obliged to carry out the wishes of her late husband, whose instructions were that in the event of his death his son should not be kept at home but sent to the cadet school. So she entered him at the school and with her daughter Varvara moved to St Petersburg in order to be near her son and to take him out at holidays.

The boy was remarkable for his brilliant ability and colossal ambition, qualities which took him to the top of his class both in his school work (particularly in mathematics on which he was especially keen) and in drill and horse-riding. Although more than usually tall, he was lithe and handsome. In conduct, too, he would have been a model cadet, had it not been for his quick temper. He did not drink or go in for debauchery; he was remarkably upright in character. All that prevented him from being a paragon was that he was given to outbursts of anger in which he lost all control of himself and became like a wild animal. On one occasion he practically threw another cadet out of a window for poking fun at his collection of minerals. Another time he almost came to grief: he threw a dishful of cutlets at the catering officer, attacked him and, it was said, struck him because he had gone back on his word and told a barefaced lie. He would certainly have been reduced to the ranks had it not been for the head of the cadet school who dismissed the catering offi- cer and hushed the matter up.

When he was eighteen Kasatsky passed out as an officer and joined an aristocratic guards regiment. The Emperor Nicholas had known him when he was still a cadet and continued to take notice of him now that he had joined his regiment, so it was predicted that he would become an imperial *aide-de-camp*. And this was Kasatsky's own earnest desire, not just because he was ambitious, but also—and chiefly—because ever since his days as a cadet he had passionately—literally passionately—loved the emperor. Every time that Nicholas visited the cadet school (which he did often), as soon as his tall, military-coated figure with swelling chest, aquiline nose, moustache and trimmed side-whiskers strode in and boomed a greeting to the cadets, Kasatsky felt the rapture of a lover, the same feeling he experienced later on meeting the woman he loved. Only his rapturous affection for Nicholas was stronger. He wanted to demonstrate the utterness of his devotion, to sacrifice something, his whole self, for him. And Nicholas was aware that he aroused this ecstasy and purposely evoked it. He played with the cadets, gathered them round him, and varied his treatment of them, being one moment boyishly simple, then friendly, then solemnly majestic. After the recent episode involving Kasatsky and the officer Nicholas said nothing to him, but when

Kasatsky came near he theatrically rebuffed him, frowned and wagged his finger. Then, as he was going, he said:

"Understand that I am aware of everything. Certain things, however, I do not wish to know. But they are here!"

He pointed to his heart.

When the cadets appeared before Nicholas on passing out, he made no further mention of this, but said, as always, that each of them could approach him directly, that they should loyally serve him and their fatherland, and that he would always be their best friend. They were all, as always, moved by this, and Kasatsky, recalling the past, shed tears and swore to serve his beloved tsar with all his strength.

When Kasatsky joined his regiment, his mother and sister moved first to Moscow and then to the country. Kasatasky gave half his property to his sister, keeping for himself only sufficient to pay his way in the smart regiment in which he served.

Outwardly Kasastsky appeared to be a perfectly ordinary brilliant young guards officer making his career, but within him there was an intense and complex process at work. Ever since childhood he had had this impulse; it had taken various apparent forms, but basically it was always the same—the urge to attain perfection and success in everything that it fell to him to do and thus attract the praise and wonder of other people. If it was a matter of study and learning he buckled down and worked until he was lauded and held up as an example to others. Once one subject was attained, he took on something new. So it was that he made himself top in his class; so it was that, when still a cadet, having noticed on some occasion how awkwardly he expressed himself in French he taught himself to speak it as perfectly as he did Russian; so it was that later, when he took up chess, he became an excellent player, though still only a cadet.

Apart from his general vocation in life, which was to serve the tsar and his country, he always had some set purpose to which, however insignificant it was, he would devote himself wholeheartedly and live only for the moment of its achievement. But no sooner had one aim been achieved than another immediately took shape in his mind and supplanted the one before. This urge to excel, and to achieve the aims he set himself in order to excel, dominated his whole life. So when he was commissioned he made it his object to achieve a complete mastery of his duties and soon became an exemplary officer, though he still suffered from the same uncontrollable temper which in his service life too caused him to do things which were bad in themselves and prejudicial to his career. Once, later, when conversing on some social occasion, he had been conscious of his lack of general education, so he determined to make good this deficiency, got down to his books and achieved what he intended. He decided then to win for himself a brilliant place in high society, became an excellent dancer, and was soon invited to all the society balls and to certain receptions as well. But this did not satisfy him. He was used to being first, and in the social world he was far from that.

High society at that time consisted (as, indeed, I think it consists at all times and in all places) of four kinds of people: (1) the wealthy who attend court; (2) the not wealthy who nonetheless have been born and brought up in court circles; (3) the wealthy who fawn on those at court; and (4) the not wealthy, unconnected with the court, who fawn on those in the first and second categories. Kasatsky did not belong to the first group, though he was readily received in the last two circles. On his very first entry into the social world Kasatsky set his sights on forming a liaison with some society lady and, contrary to his expectations, it was not long before he succeeded. But he very quickly saw that the circles in which he moved were the lower circles of society and that there were circles above these and that, though he was received in these higher court circles, he did not belong there. People were polite, but everything in their manner made it clear that he was not one of their set. And this Kasatsky wished to be. But for this it was necessary to be an *aide-de-camp* (which he had hopes of becoming) or to marry into the circle. And that is what he decided to do. The girl he selected was beautiful and one of the court circle; she was not only part of that society which he wished to enter, but someone whose acquaintance was actually sought after by all the highest and most established members of this higher circle. She was the Countess Korotkova. It was not merely on account of his career that Kasatsky began courting her: she was extraordinarily attractive and he was soon in love with her. At first she was distinctly chilly towards him, but then everything suddenly changed. She began to show signs of affection and her mother became particularly pressing with invitations.

Kasatsky proposed and was accepted. He was surprised how easily he had won such happiness; he was surprised, too, by something peculiar and odd in the behaviour of both mother and daughter towards him. He was deeply in love and blinded by his feelings and so was unaware of what practically everyone else in the city knew: that the year before his fiancée had been Nicholas's mistress.

TWO WEEKS BEFORE the day fixed for their wedding Kasatsky was sitting at his fiancée's summer villa at Tsarskoe Selo. It was a hot day in May. The engaged couple had been walking in the garden and now sat on a bench in the shade of a lime avenue. Mary was looking more than usually pretty in a white muslin dress and seemed a picture of innocence and love. She sat with lowered head, looking up now and then at the great handsome man who was talking to her with particular tenderness and caution, fearing that his every word and gesture might injure or defile the angelic purity of his betrothed. Kasatsky was one of those men of the 'forties—not met with today—who, while consciously allowing themselves to be unchaste in sexual matters and inwardly seeing nothing wrong in it, nonetheless expected their wives to possess an ideal celestial purity; they assumed this quality to exist in all the girls of their society and behaved towards them accordingly. There was much that was false in this attitude and much that was harmful in the dissolution indulged in by the men, but as far as the women were concerned this attitude—so different from that of young people today who see in every girl a female looking for a mate—was, I think, beneficial. Seeing themselves worshipped, girls actually tried to be more or less like goddesses. This attitude towards women was shared by Kasatsky, and it was thus that he regarded his bride-to-be. He was especially in love that day; he felt no sensual attraction towards her, but regarded her rather with tender awe as something unattainable.

He rose to his full height and stood before her with his hands resting on his sabre.

"It is only now that I have discovered how happy a man can be. And it is you, you—my dear," he said with a bashful smile, "that I have to thank for this."

He was still at the stage of being unused to addressing her affectionately, and to him, conscious of his moral inferiority to this angel, it seemed terrible that he should do so.

"I have come to know myself through you, . . . dear, and I have found that I am better than I thought."

"I have known it long since. That is the reason why I love you."

A nightingale trilled nearby; a sudden breeze rustled the young leaves.

He took her hand and kissed it. Tears came into his eyes. She understood that he was thanking her for saying that she loved him. He walked a little in silence, then came and sat down.

"You know, my dear, at first I had an ulterior motive in getting to know you. I wanted to form connections in society. But then, when I came to know you, how trivial that was in comparison with you! This does not make you angry?"

She made no answer, but merely touched his hand with hers. He understood its meaning: "No, I am not angry."

"You said just now . . . ," he broke off, feeling it was too much of a liberty. "You said that you love me, but—forgive me—I believe there is something else, too, which troubles you and stands in your way. What is it?"

It's now or never, she thought. He is bound to find out anyway. And he will not cry off now. Oh, but how terrible if he did!

She looked lovingly at his large, noble, powerful

figure. She loved him more than Nicholas now and, but for Nicholas being emperor, she would not have preferred him to Kasatsky.

"Listen. I cannot be untruthful and must tell you everything. You ask me what is the matter. It is that I loved someone before."

She pleadingly put her hand on his. He did not speak.

"You want to know who it was? It was him, the emperor."

"But we all love him. When you were at school, I suppose . . ."

"No, it was after. It was an infatuation, then I got over it. But I must tell you . . ."

"Well, what?"

"That there was more to it."

She covered her face with her hands.

"What? You gave yourself to him?"

She said nothing.

"You were his mistress?"

She said nothing.

He leapt to his feet and stood before her pale as death, his face quivering. He remembered now the kindly greeting Nicholas had given him when he met him on the Nevsky.

"My God! What have I done, Steve?"

"Don't touch me, don't touch me! Oh, how insufferable!"

He turned and went to the house. There he met her mother.

"What is it, Prince? I . . ." Seeing his face, she stopped. Suddenly he flushed with rage.

"You knew about this and were going to use me as a cover. If you were not both women . . . ," he cried, raising his enormous fist over her—then he turned and fled.

If the man who had been his fiancée's lover had been a private citizen he would have killed him. But it was his adored tsar.

The next day he took leave from his duties and

resigned his commission. To avoid seeing anyone he said that he was ill, and went to the country.

He spent the summer on his estate putting his affairs in order. At the end of the summer he did not return to St Petersburg, but went to the monastery which he entered as a monk.

His mother wrote trying to dissuade him from such a decisive step. He replied that the call of God was more important than any other consideration, and that he felt this call. Only his sister, who was as proud and ambitious as her brother, understood him.

She understood that he had become a monk in order to be superior to those who wanted to demonstrate their superiority over him. And she understood him correctly. By becoming a monk he was showing his scorn for all those things which seemed so important to others and which had seemed so important to him when he was an officer; he was placing himself on a new eminence from which he could look down on the people he had previously envied. But he was swayed not by this feeling alone, as his sister thought. Within him there was another, truly religious feeling of which she knew nothing, a feeling which, mingled with his pride and desire for supremacy, now governed him. His disillusionment with Mary (his fiancée), whom he had supposed so angelic, and his sense of injury were so strong that he was brought to despair, and despair brought him——to what? To God and to the faith of his childhood which had remained intact within him.

Edmund Wilson

THE ROMANCE OF OLD ST. PETERSBURG

THURSDAY, MAY 23, *Leningrad.* Intourist sign, porters; long wait like the army. Boat had arrived earlier than announced. Officials all drove away in a bus, leaving us still waiting; crowds, drab looking, but as if city belonged to them. Touched by Intourist sign when I first arrived at breakfast: "An old Russian custom: to wait. Are you from

---

American critic Edmund Wilson was an editor and writer for Vanity Fair *in the 1920s and* The New Yorker *in the 1940s. He was the author of numerous books of literary criticism, and championed the work of many now-great writers, including his good friend, F. Scott Fitzgerald. Wilson also traveled constantly; here he reports on Leningrad from a posthumous collection,* The Thirties.

the States?" (An American I met in the restaurant.) Complications about [Valentine] Stenich (Dos Passos's translator); VOKS, with Brecht, confused with man in my room named Valentine, I left him note in Brecht's room—Muriel Draper. Tretyakov[I] spoke to me at desk about Stenich, [I understood him to say] he was Brecht, asked me if I knew his book, then vanished. —*Otello:* much impressed by audience, never saw such enthusiasm, walked around in a circle in a room under the statue of Lenin: I was moved by it—the hand extended as if he were at once giving the worker what they had made and opening out the future to humanity to make whatever they could conceive. Long intermissions, during which they eat snacks and drink beer and tea. Usher left over from the old regime who asked me for money for the program—I gave him a dollar to change, which was all I had, and he brought me back six roubles—then brought me a pair of opera glasses, bowing with his hand flat on his chest such as I had never seen done—he was like a figure out of an old Russian comedy. Basy (?), who I saw between the acts, confirmed my belief that I had over-tipped him. When I got back to the hotel, I found Muriel [Draper] and Mme Litvinov,[2] had cocoa, talk with Muriel afterwards.—People going along in slippers, they seem to be particularly short on shoes. Anti-religious museum as soon as I arrived, malachite columns, lapis lazuli, lots of gold: Greek Orthodox Church Byzantine and creepy, anti-religious exhibit creepy, too pogroms and religious persecutions, propaganda exhibition, Fascism and Lenin's *Iskra,* quotations from Lenin—pendulum hanging from high dome, mummies of Metropolitan and of Siberian tsars of small tribes, Bruno, Galileo before the Inquisition. (St. Isaac's Cathedral.) —Beggar in street sur-prised me: people who don't work they won't compel to work (as somebody told me). —*Antiquités des vieux palais.* —Pretty little girl guide from Caucasus, admired *Picture of Dorian Gray.*

$2 FOR OPERA glasses, which I declined. —People at opera better dressed than people in street.

Clever girl guide on recent political events. —
Guide spoke of the Imperialist War: it inspires one
almost with awe to think how one man, Lenin, has
stamped his thought and his language on a whole people.

M. SAID THERE had been on exodus from there
recently.

May 24. Peter-Paul Fortress in morning. Old-
fashioned prison with big rooms, which didn't seem as
bad as American prisons—but everything perfectly quiet,
guards wore soft shoes, walked up and down corridors
and looked every five minutes through slot in door—
Kropotkin's cell, Vera Figner's[3] cell, cell of woman revolu-
tionist who set her hair afire with kerosene from lamp and
killed herself in that way—dark cell where they were sent
for punishment and usually went mad. Nobody had ever
escaped—the prisoners had numbers, and when their family
came to see them, the authorities said they didn't know
their names, only the numbers. Little room where Lenin's
mother had last interview with eldest son just before he

was hanged. Code alphabet: they stood against the wall with their hands behind them, so that the guards wouldn't know what they were doing: Kropotkin told the man in the cell next to him the story of the Paris Commune. — Church inside the fortress and just a little way from the prison: gold altar and columns with gold capitals, white marble tombs of the Tsars, each with a heavy gold cross on top—two made of different kinds of precious colored stone, fraudulently represented at the time as having been donated by loving peasants. Women explaining to children that the Tsars had been appointed to rule, not on account of their ability, but simply because they were sons of other Tsars. Something sinister and desolate about Leningrad: the places and public buildings that seem to go on for miles and miles—the churches like these are horrible—I don't blame them for hating their clergy. And there is something somehow not good even about the Hermitage: the most unpleasing great gallery I have ever seen—enormous canvases plastered on the walls, sometimes in three tiers, Schneyder, Rubens, arranged with no taste, vast high rooms. Catherine's present to Potemkin: cage of glass and gold with gold peacock that spreads its tail and displays it, and gold cock that crows while a little tune of bells is played—also, clock that has an enormous music box and plays eighteenth-century music from vast prickly cylinders on the hour. —*Esmeralda* in the evening. One of the Eisenstein boys estimated, apparently somewhat extravagantly, that I had tipped usher 65 to 70 roubles. That night he recognized me (the usher) and bowed low: I have apparently bought *Bittes* for as long as I stay—thrust opera glasses on me in intermission: "You keep, *bitte.*" Beer and cheese sandwich, with only one slice of bread. I kept sitting in my seat after the final curtain, as if expecting the U.S. Marines to come in and save Esmerald—M. said it would be funny if Wilson and Baker had sat in those same seats. —On the way back to the hotel, we crossed the street in the wrong place, and the people who were waiting on the curb became indignant and protested, somebody said we were "badly educated" (as Muriel explained to me)—a man followed us, still protesting, but the other people told him he was tight. —Stenich had called up in afternoon, and just as I was about to make an appointment to see him, we were cut off and I never heard from him again. —One of the Eisenstein boys told about how he had gotten into the Winter Palace on the pretense of being with a delegation— when they found he was not with the delegation, they put him out and made him come in again properly. Mrs Litvinov explained the story to us and said, "He thinks that's a joke!" They had been picked out for their ability and were getting a kind of two-year general cultural improvement. One of them very good-looking in American-looking clothes. —One's feeling toward the Soviets protective—strange effect of abolition of bourgeoisie—still true that it's not possible to be neutral. Proletariat on the signs of classless society. —Women's flat shoes, a few get high-heeled ones, which don't look very smart.

—Competition between Moscow and Leningrad betrayed by Leningrader guide's not being certain, though she had often wondered, whether Red Square in Moscow was bigger than the square in front of the Winter Place.

—M. and I had late supper at Europa after the theater: when the couples began to dance, she said it looked like the Taft in New Haven or something of the kind. They have only been allowed to dance for about three years, and they learn the steps carefully and perform them very seriously. "Jazz" looks very funny transliterated into Russian: **джаз**—Her brother-in-law in England had tried to make her take a machine for making cream out of melted butter—wondered how she could go to country which had executed a whole royal family.

—Women working with men on the street; paid the same.

May 25. Futile efforts to get Stenich on phone: they couldn't tell whether his number, as he had written it, had a 9 or an 8—girl insisted on calling 8, which was busy and didn't answer. —Red Flag textile factory: pressure, no doubt, but no such pressure, so far as I could see, as with us—they have Robert Owen's method of keeping the workers up to scratch: they are divided into brigades, each with a chief, whom they elect—the brigades compete and the names of all the members are posted on a blackboard at the end of the aisle with the amount of work each has done—those who fall behind are not punished but their names are posted to make their ignominy public. The best ones get special privileges, theater tickets, longer vacations, their photographs (in the case of the girls) posted on a background of red; skilled workers paid more than unskilled. Propaganda posters: the German working class manacled (a great red giant) and held in a barbed-wire enclosure by a snarling Nazi—to remind them of what they were being urged on for and of the danger to the working class outside. Little technical bookshop; dining room where they seemed to be eating black bread and cabbage soup. An hour for lunch. Woman with her head sunk on her arm at a table. Radio concert during intermission: two girls practicing ballet in the aisle; two more seen through the window outside in the courtyard. Seven hours a day; six hours, in the hot dyeing room—disagreeable work brings special privileges (Fourier). Here they [wear] still rather simple and inelegant clothes which you see the people in the streets wearing.

When I got back to hotel, called up Stenich—girl (Dostoevsky on buns) thought it was 8, which was out of order, so I make her try 9 and I got him: he said, "You are hard to get." Appointment for six. —Conversation with him at six: he arrived promptly—lucid and dressed à l'américaine—confusion, however, again: understood him to ask me whether I had anything to do the next evening—if not, he would take me around—then it turned out it was for tonight he was asking me. I tried to pin it down to one or the other, but he said finally, today is tomorrow. I tried again, but began to get that way myself and said (the base of the conversation had been English, but with a sprinkling of other languages), "Today, hier, heute!"—"Aujourd'hui," he corrected me. He suggested eight o'clock; I said, "All right: eight"; but he hastily added, as if things were getting too definite: "Six or nine, if you would like better!" He arrived again promptly at eight and took me to *Peter the Great* [by Alexéy Tolstóy] in the magnificent Empire gold-and-white theater, with the box all over gold for the Tsar. As I watched the expensive and brilliant production, I began to wonder whether there wasn't a political significance, and at last, when the attempted assassination took place, Stenich whispered to me, "Here certain historical parallels start." He said that A. Tolstoy was about their best writer. Stalin admires Peter the Great. Tolstoy and President of Leningrad Soviet there, a short man with black beard and sharp-pointed mustaches. All the writers by invitation in special section. Reflections on the writers; reflections on Peter; reflections on the popularity of Dos—Jimmy Herf (in *Manhattan Transfer*), and Elaine, Stenich told me, as well known as any characters of Pushkin's; reflections on factory. Soviets and U.S.A. both straining industrially for entirely different reasons—the whole thing entirely undesirable. Dos Passos's characters up against industrialism the same as the people in Russia—things that are the same, things that are different—what you can't understand unless you come here. —Walk by Neva—Stenich loved Leningrad—born there and lived there all his life, but soon there would be nothing left but factories and museums. —He was moving out to Moscow. Square of the victims of the revolution—"so quiet here you could sleep." He had been in the Red Guard, present at the taking of the Winter Palace, had known Lenin. Writers still left in Leningrad went around intoxicated by Pushkin and Dostoevsky. We talked amid the desolate long perspectives, leaning against the stone parapet of the Neva. Dark palace of the Grand Duke Constantine, uncle of the late Tsar—"He was a poet—was quite a good poet"—signed himself C.R., Constantine Romanov, he was killed. I asked how they had filled those huge palaces—he smiled, shrugged, didn't know— Constantine had had a large family, many servants. —Of the city, "Ain't it beautiful?" —Writers better off, I am told, even than engineers, the real elite—pretty soft for the writers, but is it necessarily a good thing? —Stenich would love to go to N.Y.—wants to know whether Roosevelt isn't a great man—reflections on interview with W. (?) as contrasted with supposed admiration for Roosevelt. In the midst of all this, every once in a while, old parties likely to pop up with long beards, senile, childlike, and sweet—I suppose the Soviets take the irreclaimable ones and plant them in and around the tourist hotels, making that much concession to capitalist-tourist corruption and the picturesqueness of old Russia—international chambermaids, who speak German and French.

—M. had taken little Intourist guide to opera—girl had demurred at first, because she didn't have the clothes—then, when she went, didn't want to go out between the acts.

May 26. No sightseeing. Walk with M.—M.'s attempt to see Meyerhold's *Dame aux Camélias.* It began with two sailors shaking hands—it was a ship and C.'s lovers began swarming up in groups—she thought it was a novel interpretation, but such was her respect for Meyerhold that she never questioned it—though there were more lovers than M. had ever remembered Camille's having—they seemed to have grouped themselves in factions—no doubt. Those who loved her because she could talk and those who loved her because she could listen, those who loved her because she was virtuous and those who loved her because she wasn't virtuous, etc. —Finally, she came in as if she had been shot offstage, and died. It turned out that it had been *The Optimistic Tragedy* at the Kamerny. —We walked past a number of bookshops—what libraries they evoked, as she said—to Finland Station: statue of Lenin—we sat down in the little park, and a young couple who had been sitting on the bench moved away—M. said they were afraid to have anything to do with foreigners. —Streets always being cleaned with hose—people in streets very nice when asked to direct you, etc.

—Meyerhold's new version of *Píkovaya Dama*—we sat in box—wonderful production, fine fable, which I had never appreciated before, very Russian—old Countess built up to in new production instead of being introduced in the first scene. —Looking out the window of the electric-lighted director's room with its gold Empire sphinxes and classical figures on brown polished wood, I saw the day still light at nine, the cobbled street and an old woman sitting sewing in the doorway of a great shabby yellow stucco building. —Harsh satisfactory trumpets bursting out at the ends of the scenes—mime watched by the old lady. —Harold Clurman. Shostakovich[4]—shy little sandy-colored man, with unobtrusive glasses—Miss Wright, bad monkey mouth with prominent teeth, which she has compensated for by intensification of eyes, quite attractive in spite of flat shoes—physiologist and translating Mark Twain, had fallen out with Stenich over his translation of Dos, excellent English—on *Peter the Great.* —Mayakovsky's girlfriend sitting in front of me—didn't know about her and didn't notice her. —Afterwards, caviar and vodka. —Went to bed full of Pushkin and the romance of old St. Petersburg—romance of old decanter with cockeyed top full, of water appropriate for biological cultures—story of Gorky going to factory, everything wonderfully efficient and perfect: he inquired what was made there, and was told that they made signs saying: Lift out of order.

[1]Tretyakov, author of the play *Roar, China!*, and Bertolt Brecht, author of *Threepenny Opera*.

[2]Ivy Litvinov, English wife of the Soviet foreign minister Maxim Litvinov, later ambassador to the United States.

[3]Figner (1852–1942) spent twenty years in solitary confinement for her part in the assassination of Tsar Alexander II in 1881.

[4]Clurman, EW's former New York neighbor, was in Russia at this time; Shostakovich, the Russian composer, had by this time achieved renown in the United States.

Alexander Pushkin

THE BRONZE HORSEMAN

A HUNDRED YEARS have passed, and the young city,
The glory of this northern land,
Rises in proud magnificence
From the dark forests, from the marsh and bog . . .
Along these busy banks are ranged
Massive and graceful palaces and towers,
And ships from every corner of the earth

Alexander Pushkin is the author of dozens of plays and novels, including the masterpieces Boris Gudunov *and* The Queen of Spades. *But the nineteenth-century writer is really known as Russia's greatest poet. The* Bronze Horseman, *one of his greatest verses, is dedicated to the spirit of his hometown.*

Hasten to these richly laden quays.
The Neva now wears a granite mantle,
The waters are spanned by many bridges.
The islands are dark green, garden-covered;
And our ancient Moscow perforce must yield
To the young capital which now holds sway,
As the royal widow, purple-clad, gives place
To the new Empress . . .
How fair thou art, O city of Peter,
Standing unshakeable, like Russia herself!

Acknowledgments

"Verses about Petersburg" from *The Complete Poems of Anna Akhmatova* by Anna Akhmatova. Translated by Judith Hemschemeyer ©1990, 1992. Reprinted by permission of Zephyr Press.

Excerpt from *The Italics Are Mine* by Nina Berberova ©1991 by Chatto & Windus, Ltd., ©1969 by Nina Berberova. Translated by P. Radley. Reprinted by permission of Alfred A. Knopf Inc.

Excerpt from *Soviet Women: Walking the Tightrope* by Francine du Plessix Gray ©1990 by Francine du Plessix Gray. Reprinted by permission of Doubleday Books.

Excerpt from *Russian Journal* by Andrea Lee ©1981 by Andrea Lee. Reprinted by permission of Random House, Inc.

Excerpt from *Most Beloved* by Tatyana Tolstaya ©1991 by Tatyana Tolstaya. Reprinted by permission of Vintage Books, a division of Random House.

Excerpt from *Father Sergius* by Leo Tolstoy, translated by Paul Foote. ©1977 by Paul Foote. Reprinted by permission of Penguin Books, a division of Viking Penguin USA.

Excerpt from *The Romance of Old St. Petersburg* by Edmund Wilson ©1980 by Helen Miranda Wilson. Reprinted by permission of Random House, Inc.